Gaia's Gift

Turning traditional theology upside down, Primavesi offers an earth-centred vision that is liberating and profoundly hopeful. Written with eloquence and clarity, *Gaia's Gift* is the most up-to-date theological response to the challenge of science. A tour de force!

Kwok Pui-lan, *Episcopal Divinity School, Massachusetts*

Once again this unique and important thinker breaks new ground. Primavesi brings her distinctive blend of critical acumen, cross-disciplinary savvy and ethical passion to bear upon the interface of cutting-edge theology and radical science.

Gwen Griffith-Dickson,
Gresham College and Birkbeck College, University of London

Gaia's Gift, the second of Anne Primavesi's explorations of human relationships with the earth, asks that we complete the ideological revolution set in motion by Copernicus and Darwin concerning human importance. They challenged the notion of our God-given centrality within the universe and within earth's evolutionary history. Yet as our continuing exploitation of earth's resources and species demonstrates, we remain wedded to the theological assumption that these are there for our sole use and benefit. Now James Lovelock's scientific understanding of the existential reality of Gaia's gift of life again raises the question of our proper place within the universe. It turns us decisively towards an understanding of ourselves as dependent on, rather than in control of, the whole earth community.

Anne Primavesi is the author of *Sacred Gaia* (Routledge, 2000), and a former Research Fellow in Environmental Theology at the University of Bristol.

Gaia's Gift

Earth, Ourselves and God After Copernicus

Anne Primavesi

Routledge
Taylor & Francis Group

LONDON AND NEW YORK

First published 2003 by Routledge
11 New Fetter Lane, London EC4P 4EE

Simultaneously published in the USA and Canada
by Routledge
29 West 35th Street, New York, NY 10001

Routledge is an imprint of the Taylor & Francis Group

Typeset in Galliard by Wearset Ltd, Boldon, Tyne and Wear
Printed and bound in Great Britain by TJ International Ltd, Padstow,
Cornwall

British Library Cataloguing in Publication Data
A catalogue record for this book is available from the British Library

Library of Congress Cataloging in Publication Data
Primavesi, Anne, 1934–
    Gaia's gift : earth, ourselves, and God after Copernicus / Anne
Primavesi.
        p. cm.
    Includes bibliographical references and index.
    1. Religion and science—History. 2. Man (Christian theology)—
History of doctrines. 3. Human ecology—Religious aspects—
Christianity. 4. Gaia hypothesis. I. Title.

BL245.P75 2003
291.2′4—dc21

                                                                    2002037162

ISBN 0–415–28834–7 (hbk)
ISBN 0–415–28835–5 (pbk)

For Mark: Gaia's gift to me

Contents

Acknowledgements

For reasons that will, I hope, become increasingly clear throughout this book, I want now to formally acknowledge Earth's primary contribution to it as to every other human enterprise. The priority given to Earth in the book's subtitle makes the same point. However, it will also be abundantly clear that in fact we consistently accord priority to ourselves over Earth – usually on the grounds that God has given it to us or that our intellect entitles us to it.

That said, there are smaller and more obvious debts of gratitude to be registered too. I and all my readers will want to thank Cornelia Durrant for volunteering, in her own words, to be my 'prize chump': a role usually reserved for the man on top of the Clapham omnibus. It meant that she read the chapters as I wrote them and then told me whether or not they made sense. Any remaining senselessness is, then, due solely to me and to my inability to recognize it. My debt to Jim Lovelock is clearly evident, as is that due to Glynn Gorick, not only for another beautiful cover illustration but also for his thought-provoking response to *Sacred Gaia*. Countless friends, here and in Ireland, have contributed valuable insights and corrections at different stages, notably Mary Midgley, Joan Solomon, Colin Carr, Dorothea McEwan and Edward James. Mark, my husband, has contributed at every stage, most obviously in compiling the index with loving care and attention.

I am grateful to Birkbeck College for a research grant that enabled me to consult relevant sources in a variety of libraries. And once again I acknowledge my debt to the editorial staff at Routledge. Roger Thorp commissioned this book before Julene Knox took over from him as editor. She encouraged and supported me until she too left. A special word of thanks then to Clare Johnson, who saw the book safely through from commission to publication. She has been not only professionally resourceful but also cheerfully and patiently helpful.

My thanks to Faber and Faber for giving me non-exclusive English language permission throughout the UK and British Commonwealth to quote on p. 86 here from *The Planet on the Table* from *The Collected Poems of Wallace Stevens*. The permission from Alfred A. Knopf to reproduce the poem elsewhere in the world is given on that same page exactly as they require.

Introduction

When a telegraph cable was to be laid for the first time between Great Britain and the United States, it was immensely important to know the exact nature of the bottom of the sea so as to guard against the costly cable being frayed or cut. So in 1857 the Admiralty commissioned a survey of the seabed over the whole line of the cable. Thomas Huxley had specimens from the survey sent to him for analysis, and found that almost the whole of the central plain beneath the North Atlantic, from Valentia on the west coast of Ireland to Trinity Bay in Newfoundland, was covered by a fine chalky mud that, when brought to the surface, dried into a greyish-white substance. If you are so inclined, you can write with it on a blackboard, as he did in his 1868 lecture, *On a Piece of Chalk*. Huxley said that when he examined a section of this substance under the microscope, he saw congregated together innumerable minute chambered skeletal bodies, beautifully constructed of calcium carbonate in a variety of coccolith forms and on average not larger than a hundredth of an inch across.

Similar skeletons, he remarked, were being formed in the sea even as he spoke, as they are now. They form around subvisible living organisms and when these die the skeletons rain down thousands of feet (part of the phenomenon called 'marine snow') to become part of the deep sea mud on the ocean floor. Over a very long period of time this deposit builds up until, over an even longer period, it is upheaved into coastal landscapes – a process that once formed the white cliffs of Dover.

In contrast to Huxley's research into the formation of deep sea mud, his great friend, Charles Darwin, devoted the last years of his life to studying the superficial layer of earth that we call top soil. He discovered during the course of his studies that worms created the earth: that is, this layer of organic material mixed with disintegrated rock in which plants grow. The results of the earthworms' labour startled him sufficiently for him to ask how human work compares with that done through their agency. He felt that we needed 'to shuffle the traditional hierarchies': not so much by diminishing ourselves but by trying to fit our proper size. Huxley had a rather similar reaction to the organisms that helped create the chalk – on the surface of which we too can now see earthworms continuing their creative labours (Primavesi 2002: 26).

Whatever Darwin had in mind when he called for traditional hierarchies to be 'shuffled', we now have a clearer idea of his own contribution to this process. Stephen Jay Gould throws some light on it when he quotes Freud's remark that each major science has made one signal contribution to the reconstruction of human thought – and that each step in this painful progress has shattered yet again an original hope for our own transcendent importance in the universe. Humanity has had to endure, Freud said, from Copernicus and Darwin, 'two great outrages upon its naïve self-love. The first when it realized that our earth was not the centre of the universe. . . . The second when biological research robbed man [sic] of the particular privilege of having been specially created and relegated him to a descent from the animal world' (Gould 1987: 1).

Gould does not say when Freud made his comments, but a similar, although more positive, connection between Copernicus and Darwin was made immediately after the latter's death in 1882. In a funeral oration to the Berlin Academy entitled *Darwin und Kopernicus*, naturalist Emil Du Bois-Reymond said that, together, they had established the proper position for humanity within Nature, with Darwin finishing what Copernicus had begun. Bois-Reymond's positive assessment of their work in establishing our 'proper' position within the universe was not, however, universally accepted. Four years later Nietzsche complained that since Copernicus, humanity appeared to be rolling ever faster down an inclined plane (von Cues 1957: 7f.).

Whether positive or negative, the assessments necessarily came from within a privileged group of well-educated European men who, as Gould points out in relation to Freud, considered themselves and their own work of equal value to that of Copernicus and Darwin. This self-assessment qualified them, in their own eyes and in those of the public generally, to accept or reject any opinion put forward by science or, indeed, by religion. They exemplify those within the academic and ecclesiastical establishments who, on the basis of privileged knowledge (both in the sense of privileging those who hold it and of their being privy to it) consider themselves, and are considered by others, to be at the top of traditional pyramidal hierarchies in which, for those of a religious persuasion, humanity takes second place only to God. This notional pyramid's greatest mass, at its lowest level, is, one may safely assume, formed by those visible and subvisible non-human organisms raised to prominence by Huxley and Darwin. Any intimation of our sliding in that direction, rather than being naturally oriented upwards, would constitute a shuffling or reversal within the hierarchical order that would indeed be considered outrageous.

Gould, however, brings that outrage closer when he adds a third, contemporary step towards it to those already taken by Copernicus and Darwin: the discovery of 'deep time'; time in the biological and geological distant past. The discovery, exploration and exposition of this past in terms of interaction between living organisms and their environments had, as we have seen, excited Huxley's admiration and aroused Darwin's awe. As James Lovelock developed Gaia theory, our history came to be seen within the context of this larger whole, so establishing our proper place within it. This, for me, is the theory's major conceptual gift to the history of human thought. By examining the continuous interactions between life and environment that emerged in deep time, and evolved over billions of years into the life-support systems essential for the eventual emergence and evolution of our own species, Lovelock made it theoretically impossible for us to claim pole position in the evolution of life; or to be the exception to evolutionary rules; or to be exempt from the power of death and change.

There is now a general acceptance of our dependence on life-support systems that evolved over time in their own right. Understanding of its implications is being gradually built up through our experience of its truth in phenomena such as climate change, atmospheric pollution and loss of biodiversity: all now a cause of concern to us and incidentally a witness to our interdependence with all life forms on earth. This shift in common understanding of what our lives daily depend on has helped create conditions within our culture in which it is now possible to appreciate the most obvious feature of Gaia's gift: its existential reality. Gaia gives us the experience of being alive: one common to all living beings. This gift is given to and received by us all, just as we are, consciously or not, at every moment of our existence.

The theoretical aspect of Gaia's gift gives us concepts, such as 'tight bonding with our environments', 'self-regulation' and 'homeostasis' (to be discussed in Chapter 5) that enable us to talk about and deepen our understanding of what it means to be alive and of what supports life, whether our own or that of others. Together with the existential reality of experiencing our own bonding with the environment, the theoretical discussion and research into them makes nonsense of the notion that we as a species were created independently of the biological, chemical and geological processes that evolved throughout deep time into the present and proceed now into the future.

But what, Gould asks, could be more comforting or convenient for an assumption of human superiority and domination than the traditional concept of a young earth ruled by human will within days of its origin? And what could be more wounding to human self-importance than to find we emerged naturally from an environment which had flourished more than happily without us over billions of years (Gould 1987: 2)?

As I became more aware of the persistence of this mindset and therefore of resistance to taking the work of Copernicus, Darwin and Lovelock to its logical conclusion, I understood why evolutionary biologist William Hamilton said that the revolutionary potential of Gaia theory is in continuity with and of the same order as that of Copernicus and Darwin. The challenge posed by their work (implicit rather than expressed, as we shall see, in the case of Copernicus) to traditional hierarchical views of humanity's overwhelming importance confirmed, once again, how entrenched the traditional views are. Previous research has helped me understand how great a role Christianity has played in creating and maintaining these notional hierarchies within western culture generally, not least by presenting a particular understanding of God as architect of their pyramidal structure. This last explains why I found such resistance among theologians to the notion that we are not entitled to an exceptional place within the evolution of life on earth, one that by implication at least, would place us outside it.

By contrast, in *Sacred Gaia* I drew various conclusions about the relationship between earth, ourselves and God that did not focus solely on divine–human interactions, but presumed that God's relationship with earth encompassed all living beings, including those living on it throughout the billions of years before our species emerged. This challenged various theological presuppositions about our role and place within earth's history and was perceived, therefore, as diminishing human significance and reacted to accordingly – even though my intention was to focus on the significance of all life forms. For the idea of our centrality in earth's history, and all that flows from it, is so taken for granted as to be almost impregnable to revision in the light of new discoveries and information about our actual place and role within that history.

Hamilton's remark about Copernicus sent me back to look at what it was in a theory about the rotation of the earth around the sun that made it a decisive moment in western perceptions of our status within the whole earth community. Again, it had to do with science questioning traditional hierarchies. Copernicus asked a particular question about the earth and its place in the universe and by doing so, was perceived as asking for a complete change in how we see our position here on earth. The generally negative reaction to his suggestion that the earth is not the centre of the universe was not, I found, simply because earth's position there was threatened, but because, by implication, ours was. This tied in with a theological legacy of seeing ourselves as central to God's concerns and as God's representatives on earth. This legacy (looked at in some depth in Chapters 1 to 4) came to be seen as a writ of entitlement to human 'control' of the earth. While that presupposition usually remains unstated now, it supports the belief, even in a post-Christian culture, that we are somehow entitled to the dominant position here.

In Christian fundamentalist circles, religious entitlement to the controlling position in earth's hierarchy of life is stated and claimed openly. In *Sacred Gaia* I had assumed that Gaia theory would show up this theological presupposition for what it is: the construct of a theology of divine/human power over others; of a type of theology imaged on a male omnipotent God who gave power over the world to a human elite. This theological presupposition supports the view that God's will was, and is, that we should rule over and use the world and all living creatures within it for our own purposes, that is, for our sole use and benefit.

After Copernicus, Darwin and Lovelock, however, there is an increasingly serious scientific challenge to this presupposition that requires a serious contemporary theological response rather than a rehearsal of old pieties. Above all, it requires exposing the presuppositions about earth, ourselves and God fundamental to traditional Christian hierarchies. Some of these presuppositions are discussed in the opening chapters of this book, building on more extensive discussion in my earlier work, *From Apocalypse to Genesis: Ecology, Feminism and Christianity* (1991) and *Sacred Gaia* (2000). The emphasis here is on an extended and deepening understanding of the science of life on earth as part of an evolution, indeed a revolution in our perception of ourselves. Such a revolution would involve coming to see the nature of our humanity, in common with that of all other living beings, as emerging from and belonging to the material, chemical and physical structure of the earth, its *humus*. And to see that we are not, therefore, given exceptional status by virtue of a specially created position independent of or outside the processes that power and sustain the evolution of all life on earth. A position that, we have been led to believe, entitles us to control over it.

Within western culture as a whole, where theology has generally ceded authority over opinion to science, the theological basis for adopting this view of our place in the universe no longer has its earlier force. The relationship between them has undergone an almost complete role reversal since Copernicus's day. At that time theology had the last word. That is now presumed to belong to science. But this does not mean theology has lost all influence. It contributed positively to the Copernican revolution in that Copernicus claimed validity for his astronomical science against that of Ptolemy on theological grounds. Now, after Copernicus opened the way from a closed to an infinite universe, theology can react positively by breaking open the concept of God: from one enclosed within a relationship with us to one unconfined and undetermined by human thought, word or action.

The way to this is opened by an acknowledgement that as we belong to a heliocentric universe in which our life, in common with that of all living creatures on earth, is ultimately dependent on energy received from the sun, so too our religious experience lives out of the ultimate gift relationship in our lives: that between God and the whole community of life on earth. Sharing food is the most basic and visible form of gift exchange between ourselves and the other members of the earth community. It has also been used religiously as a symbolic exchange of gifts given to us through God's procreative love, one that evokes our deepest gratitude. And that gratitude is as valid a response as Darwin's awe or Huxley's admiration. Setting one form of gift exchange within the context of the other, rather than separating them in any absolutist fashion, enhances the value of both in our eyes. Seeing what we give to others and what is given to us within the continuing, all-encompassing community of life is a way of transcending the boundaries of any particular time and place.

This perspective on our gift relationship with God goes directly against the theological view of our species as specially created and favoured by God, a status that would place us (logically) outside Darwinian evolutionary processes. And it is this claim to human exceptionalism, entrenched in and compellingly articulated by traditional Christianity, that has, up to now, effectively blocked out the revolutionary question of our real status and role on earth. As it continues to do, even for those who neither claim nor acknowledge the visible support of ecclesiastical authority for assuming our right to the dominant position here. For it is highly congenial to our self-esteem, as Gould pointed out, to consider ourselves uniquely independent and therefore a supremely important species.

Gaia theory, however, leaves us in no doubt as to our emergence and place in evolutionary history and our dependent position within it. We depend on the earth's physical, chemical and climatic gifts to us: on its self-regulatory abilities and on the creative labours of its non-human species, living and dead, visible and subvisible, to support our existence. Lynn Margulis, Lovelock's closest early collaborator, sums up our true status by remarking that human independence is a political concept, not a scientific one. She describes the 'illusion' of independence from Nature as 'dangerous ignorance' and counters it by demonstrating the vital role of subvisible organisms in the evolution and unbroken continuum of life on earth from its inception up to the present moment (Margulis 1986: 13–23; Margulis and Sagan 1995: 26).

So while I say that Gaia theory is a conceptual gift to us, its challenging implications make it an uncomfortable, indeed unwelcome one for many. Nevertheless the need for us to come to terms with what it says about our role and place within Nature seems to me now to be in direct proportion to what we as a species have done and have assumed our right to do to the global human habitat. In *Something New Under the Sun: an Environmental History of the Twentieth-Century World*, J.R. McNeil, professor of history at Georgetown University, demonstrates, with the help of colleagues from various disciplines, that without necessarily intending it, over the course of the past century the human race has undertaken what he calls a giant, uncontrolled experiment on the earth. To a degree unprecedented in human history, we have refashioned the earth's air, water and soil along with the composition of the biosphere on which all life depends. We have become, as his tables and graphs amply illustrate, a geological force rivalling wind-erosion, glaciers, volcanoes and water; we have recast the global nitrogen and phosphorus cycles; and through these activities have altered and polluted the earth's crust and atmosphere chemically, biologically and physically (McNeil 2000).

McNeil and his co-authors demonstrate how the growth of technology (in earth-moving equipment, for example) has made these drastic changes possible. And the unrestricted growth of industrial complexes as well as gross expenditure of effort and resources on military projects raises the most pertinent question about the function of traditional hierarchies: what leads us to assume that we are entitled to make such an impact on the earth and on its life resources, causing misery to our fellow humans and the extinction of countless other species in the process?

This question of entitlement, one increasingly raised by the visible effects of our impact on the earth, needs to be taken seriously and discussed in depth by those of us who may have assumed, explicitly or implicitly, that it is answered by an appeal to a higher authority, whether religious, philosophical, economic or scientific. That assumption makes us complicit in the effects of our claiming that entitlement. Therefore we are obliged to explicitly question its legitimacy.

Who is this a question for? Not for those among us who have suffered or suffer the effects of that claim: indigenous peoples, subsistence farmers and environmental and economic refugees. Nor is it a question for those who have never seen themselves as owners or controllers of earth's resources. It is, however, being raised by their plight, and by groups attentive to it within civil society and in various religious and environmental associations and charities (Primavesi 2000: 72–120).

Those sentient beings at the bottom of traditional hierarchical pyramids who find the existential experience of Gaia's gift painful and degrading, one of deprivation rather than enrichment of life, need those of us who are able to do so to argue for its theoretical basis and scientific conclusions: to explain, in contemporary terms, that we, in common with all living beings, are gifted with life rather than in control of it. They also need those of us who have inherited traditionally religious hierarchical views of ourselves to examine, as honestly and as thoroughly as possible, the theological conclusions drawn from those religious narratives on which such views have been constructed.

The following prototypical example, which will be examined from different viewpoints throughout this book, is the biblical story of a Flood.

In the genealogy of those descended from Adam, Methuselah was the grandfather of Noah, who had three sons, Shem, Ham and Japheth. During Noah's lifetime human wickedness reached such a peak and made God so angry that he decided to put up with it no longer. He would send a flood that would blot man out from the face of the earth, as well as all beasts, creeping things and birds of the air. Every living thing would die. He would drown them all and wash them away out of his sight. But Noah had not behaved badly. So God said to him: 'Build yourself an ark of gopher wood according to my instructions, and take your wife, your sons and your sons' wives into the ark with you. Take also a breeding pair of every non-human species, and every sort of food for you and for them.'

So Noah did everything God told him. Seven days later God sent rain which fell for forty days and nights. The fountains of the great deep burst forth, and the windows of the heavens were opened. All flesh died, and all living things were blotted out. God shut Noah and all the beasts in the ark, and the waters lifted it up high above the earth. And the waters prevailed on the earth for a hundred and fifty days.

But God remembered Noah and all the beasts in the ark, and made a wind blow over the earth. The waters subsided and the fountains of the deep and the windows of the heavens were closed. In the seventh month, on the seventeenth day, the ark came to rest on the mountains of Ararat. After forty days Noah opened a window in the ark and sent out a raven. Then he sent a dove, who could find no perch and returned to him. He waited another seven days, and sent her out again. This time she came back to him with a fresh olive leaf in her beak. So he knew then that the waters had gone down. Seven days later he sent her out again, and this time she did not return.

So Noah removed the cover from the ark and looked out himself. And the ground was dry. God told him to leave the ark, taking his family with him as well as all the other creatures, clean and unclean. Then Noah sacrificed some of the clean animals and birds. This pleased God, who said that he would never again curse the earth because of the bad things man did. God told Noah he would have many descendants, as would his children, and that every bird of the air and every beast on the ground and all the fish of the sea were delivered into his hands. They would fear and dread both him and his descendants. Everything that lives and moves was to be food for him, and all the green plants were given to him. In fact, everything was given to him except the lifeblood of other men and their brothers. For God said: 'Whoever sheds the blood of man, by man shall his blood be shed. *For God made man in his own image.*'

(Genesis 6–9. My italics)

The dénouement of this particular narrative, as well as the dramatic action leading up to it, reveals some salient features and major characters in the hierarchical construct of our relationship with God. Earth, its resources and its creatures feature solely as the stage on which we act out that relationship. The ark is built as a joint God–man enterprise. A male God confirms the patriarch's exceptional status by ensuring his escape from a catastrophic natural disaster (initiated by God) that wipes out almost all living creatures. Earth is also the place, we are reminded, where God created Adam, Noah's ancestor from whom (through Noah) we are all descended, with some (men) inheriting his rights and privileges because they are made in God's image.

In the case of both Adam and Noah, God's wrath at human sin has consequences for all other creatures. In Adam's case, all are condemned to suffer death. In Noah's case, some creatures (chosen by him) have their sentence of death temporarily suspended. In each instance the male human being is the focus of God's wrath, or love: but always the decisive figure in God's relationship with the whole world.

In this particular episode, under God's direction human shelters are destroyed or built, fountains and clouds burst open or close, waters raise or lower themselves. Noah chooses certain creatures for a controlled breeding programme and when they emerge from the ark classifies them, on his own criteria, as 'clean' and 'unclean'. He chooses some 'clean' ones as victims, that is, as sacrifices to God. Their sacrifice 'pleases' God, who in response promises not to curse the earth again because of human misdeeds. God also promises Noah many descendants, and delivers all earth's creatures and produce into his hands. Noah is given absolute power, power of life and death, over every living thing, except his fellow men. Human life alone is sacrosanct, because man is made in God's image.

God has, it is true, in most contemporary revisions of the story, lost the director's chair to Noah, or rather, to a few of his descendants. Now, however, earth itself, and *all* its creatures, is moving centre stage under a spotlight focused on it by Gaia theory and the earth sciences. Perhaps, before it is too late, we may perceive that it is only in the light illuminating earth as a whole that we may truly see ourselves.

1 The astronomical revolution

The year 1543 saw the publication of *De Revolutionibus Orbium Coelestium* (*On the Revolutions of the Celestial Spheres*) and the death of its author, Nicholas Copernicus. He received the first printed copy of the work on his death-bed. For some historians this work marks the end of the Middle Ages and the beginning of modern times. However, in his study of the period, *The Astronomical Revolution*, Alexander Koyré wonders if we ought not to go further and say that the break caused by the work of Copernicus lies between us and, not only the Middle Ages, but classical antiquity too. For, he says, 'only since the time of Copernicus has man ceased to be the centre of the Universe, and the Cosmos ceased to be regulated around him' (Koyré 1973: 15f.).

If this de-centring of man had indeed pervaded European consciousness, and if all that follows from it had become an accomplished fact, as Koyré seems to imply, this book would be unnecessary. But on the contrary we now live in an even more homocentric, that is, man-centred universe than the pre-Copernican one.[1] Certainly our impact on the earth itself, and indeed on our solar system, is far, far greater. For our reach now encompasses not only most of the earth's surface but extends to the earth's atmosphere, and beyond that even to the moon. Beyond that again a three-year mission to investigate the nature of solar emissions is now underway. The theoretical, astronomical Copernican revolution that put the sun at the centre of our universe has, it is true, largely been completed so that we may routinely distinguish between the sun's apparent motion around us (apparent, that is, to us) and the real motion of the earth. But the difference between our apparent supremacy on earth and our real place there has made hardly any impression on our consciousness or on the scope of our activities, despite the best efforts of environmentalists and groups committed to raising awareness of their effects.

There are many reasons for this failure of consciousness, some of which can be discerned in the reactions to the original astronomical Copernican revolution. They now appear predictable, given the social, religious and scientific context in which Copernicus lived and worked. However, in spite of the fact that we appear to have moved far beyond them in many ways, they are still recognizably present in our own time. To judge both our distance from him and from his context, and at the same time see the continuity between that period and our own, we need to look at his context in rather more detail.

For a start, this means forgetting the intellectual development of the centuries after Copernicus and imagining that we, and everyone else, believe, with absolute confidence based on the shared evidence of our senses, *that the Earth does not move*. However, the sun and other planets apparently do move – around the Earth. Everything in the universe revolves around our planet and so around us. We, as the predecessors of Copernicus, see that we live in a geocentric and a homocentric universe created as such by God.

It is here, in this milieu, that Copernicus proposes, on the sole basis of mathematical calculations necessarily understood by very few, that the Earth moves. And that it moves around the sun.

Even those who could understand why he said this found it almost impossible to accept its implications. It involved, says Koyré, the destruction of a worldview that science (in the person of Ptolemy), philosophy (in the person of Aristotle) and religion (Jewish, Christian and Islamic) represented as being centred on man and created for him.

Personal background

Unless we attempt this imaginative leap into Copernicus's world, however, it is impossible for us to realize the magnitude of his achievement or the challenge it posed to his contemporaries. Or why acceptance of its implications in regard to ourselves has been so long delayed. We must also take into account the fact that certain aspects of Copernicus's own life set him almost as far apart from the mass of his contemporaries as he is from us. In these days of electronic networks, for instance, it is hard for us to grasp the relative isolation of scholars from each other at a time when the fastest means of communication equalled the speed of the fastest horse. His scholarly circle was necessarily confined to the very few astronomers cited in Koyré's extensive notes who knew him or could understand his work. For his outstanding abilities marked him out from them at the same time as those abilities enabled him, on the evidence presented to him by his own observations and astronomical tables, to overcome the evidence of his senses and rethink the real, as opposed to the apparent, motion of the heavenly bodies.

The greatness of Copernicus, observes Koyré, does not depend on his contribution of new facts but on the conception and development of a new theory based on those available to him (Koyré 1973: 23). Very few others could, or would, understand or follow it to its unwelcome conclusions about ourselves and our place in the universe. Indeed it is probably true to say that he himself shirked facing the radical nature of those conclusions, preferring to stress the continuity of his work with that of Ptolemy. He was in fact hailed as 'the new Ptolemy'.

Which brings us to the second point to be made about him. In that period, one devoted to tradition and respect for authority, the desire for change was seen as a great sin. Any step forward had to be presented as a movement backwards, as a return to origins. So his pupil, Georg Rheticus, in the first account of Copernicus's work, insisted that in spite of his break with Ptolemy in respect to geocentrism, Copernicus had no desire to make changes. This is borne out by the fact that Kepler later reproached Copernicus with having followed Ptolemy too closely (Koyré 1973: 15f.). This respect for tradition and authority went far beyond his scientific work. It was, after all, integral to his main vocation as a Roman Catholic canon. As such, he belonged to the greatest conservative (some would say retrograde) force in Europe at that time.

Set against this cultural and personal background, something of the magnitude of his proposal (that the earth moves around the sun) begins to emerge. Its religious implications in particular, although not drawn out by him, were such that, when Galileo's use of the telescope supplied some of the empirical evidence needed to support it, the Roman Catholic Church reacted forcefully. In 1616, some seventy-three years after his death, it solemnly condemned Copernicus's work.

Few personal details are known about this extraordinary man, apart from his academic achievements. Born in 1473, he was a Polish Roman Catholic who studied at Cracow University and went on from there to study law at the University of Bologna. This was a requirement for his becoming a canon at Frauenberg Cathedral where his uncle was bishop. In 1500 he went to Rome where he lectured for a short time in mathematics (which Koyré says undoubtedly means astronomy) before returning to Frauenberg to be officially installed in his canonry. He then asked for leave of absence and returned to Italy where, in 1503, in Padua, he received his doctorate in canon law. This extensive education also included medicine (another discipline required of a canon) and the usual subjects of a humanities course. It meant that when he did return to his canonry he led a very busy life: as secretary and assistant to his uncle, the bishop; and as a university lecturer where Georg Rheticus, his most famous pupil in astronomy, was also his chronicler (Koyré 1973: 19–23).

Given the amount of activity involved in his work as a canon, astronomy could be seen almost as a hobby. Through it, however, as a result of his own observations and mathematical calculations, he became convinced, against the prevailing wisdom, of two very important things about the shape of the world (*forma mundi*) and its inner workings (*ratio motuum machinae mundi*). The first was that the sun (not the earth) is at the centre of the universe. The second was that the earth has a twofold rotation: a daily rotation on its axis and an annual rotation, or revolution, around the sun. His chief work, *De Revolutionibus Orbium Coelestium*, was not, as we saw, published until 1543, the year of his death. He delayed publishing it because, even though it was dedicated to Pope Paul III, he rightly feared ecclesiastical censure.

So he was careful to explain in his dedication that he was not the first to believe that the earth revolves around the sun. He reminded the Pope that both Cicero and Plutarch recorded the fact that followers of Pythagoras had held that the earth moved, and that in the third century BCE a Greek astronomer, Aristarchus of Samos, thought that all the planets, including the earth, go around the sun in circles (Copernicus 1992: 3–6). Aristarchus too had advanced this view rather tentatively, since, according to Plutarch, it could have led to his indictment on the charge of impiety. Copernicus's own fear of offending religious prejudice by even proposing a heliocentric universe was, as we saw, well-founded.

The full import of his theory, as I said, became apparent only in 1610 when Galileo published an account of the discoveries he had made about Jupiter's satellites through the use of a telescope. This had a far more dramatic impact on his peers than Copernicus's mathematical speculations. Kepler's immediate response was an enthusiastic letter to Galileo saying that he longed for a telescope so that he might anticipate Galileo in discovering the satellites around Mars. Galileo's colleagues at Padua University, however, did not share Kepler's enthusiasm or eagerness to see for themselves. They refused Galileo's offer of a look through his telescope for they knew, they said, that Jupiter could not have satellites as there could not be more than seven heavenly bodies. The universe demonstrated again and again, they argued, the importance God had assigned to the number seven (see this characteristic feature in the biblical narrative at the end of the Introduction) – and if the number of planets were increased, this whole universal system would fall to the ground. It is also the case, they said, that as these satellites were invisible to the naked eye, they could not exercise any influence on the earth.

In this intellectual climate, influenced, it seems, more by astrology than by astronomy, Galileo went to Rome in 1615 to campaign for his view. However, instead of winning over the Church authorities he merely consolidated their opposition. His view was condemned as 'absurd in philosophy and formally heretical, because expressly contrary to Holy Scripture'. It was in this situation that in 1616 Copernicus's book was formally suspended by the Roman Church until it could be 'corrected' (Jones 1969: 98–102). Whether this meant its being rewritten or being falsified is open to conjecture, but the latter seems more likely as it remained on the Index of forbidden books until 1822.

It would be a mistake, however, to see religious prejudice as the only factor in the negative reactions to Copernicus or Galileo. While biblical authority was invoked by both Protestant and Roman Catholic clerics to oppose heliocentric theory and prevented its general acceptance until the beginning of the eighteenth century, it would be wrong to regard it as the only, or even chief obstacle. In fact at the time of Copernicus, and down to that of Descartes and Galileo, the entrenched position of Aristotelian philosophy and physics, opposed to his calculations, constituted an equally, if not more powerful obstacle (Koyré 1973: 72; Blumenberg 1987: 142–145). It was also the case that there were mathematical weaknesses and obscurities inherent in the Copernican system which had to be corrected by Kepler and Newton (Hallyn 1997: 89–103). Medieval church historian Heiko Oberman points out (Oberman 1986: 188) that even if there had been no religious scruples whatever against the Copernican astronomy, sensible men all over Europe, especially the most empirically minded (such as Galileo's colleagues), would have pronounced it 'a wild appeal to accept the premature fruits of an uncontrolled imagination, in preference to the solid inductions, built up gradually through the ages, of man's confirmed sense experience' (Oberman 1986: 188; Dillenberger 1988: 21f.).

Pre-Copernican worldview

It is still the case, as reactions to Lovelock's Gaia theory from some scientists show, that any worldview which is commonly held and is reasonably workable can be and will be adhered to, even against compelling evidence, as this involves no expenditure of energy or need to abandon cherished theories or ways of working. And in Copernicus's lifetime just such a view of the universe, built around the Ptolemaic system, was firmly in place. Ptolemy, an astronomer, geographer and mathematician, had lived and worked in Alexandria in the mid-second century CE. From the mathematical point of view, observes Koyré, his system is one of the finest and most outstanding works of the human mind. More importantly, it had been reconciled with the biblical picture of the world. The general outlines were clear. At the centre of the universe was the immovable planet, Earth, and beyond it a series of spheres containing the planets, including the sun and moon. The planets moved in epicycles forming a perfect circular form around the fixed earth. Hell was at the centre of the earth and spatially farthest removed from the pure Empyrean, heaven, situated beyond the spheres. This was the incorruptible dwelling place of God and the eventual abode of the redeemed.

Such a worldview could be visualized and its meaning discerned. Space and destiny coincided in it, as everything had its place and purpose. The whole universe was seen as ministering to the earth (or rather, to man). Christian doctrine developed the notion that the significance of earth's location at the centre of the universe was central to human significance as it was the place of man's dramatic redemption from Hell by Christ. This picture of the world, developed and refined through the centuries, was so integral to the perceived ends and purposes of human life that it commanded universal acceptance and could not easily be abandoned (Koyré 1973: 23f.; Dillenberger 1988: 22–24).

A graphic presentation of this worldview (which can also be seen as a later episode in the story of an idea about ourselves and God) is found in Botticelli's magnificent depiction of Dante's *Divine Comedy*. Botticelli's illustrations, drawn between 1480 and 1495 (in Copernicus's lifetime), depict the trajectory of Dante's journey from the depths of hell upward through the spheres to the Empyrean, beyond which lives the radiance of God: 'the love which moves the sun and the other stars.' In the illustration for the second canto of Dante's *Paradiso*, Botticelli includes a Ptolemaic/Aristotelian model of the cosmos: in the centre is the earth ('tera'), around it the atmosphere ('aria') and the zone of fire ('fuocho'); then the seven planetary spheres, with the sun and moon identified by symbols. Outside and beyond them is the sphere of the fixed stars, and outside that again, the Primum Mobile or crystalline heaven. To indicate the primacy of contemplation over visualization, the Empyrean is not shown. For who has seen God? The Ptolemaic diagram of the cosmos (although not referred to by Dante) is used by Botticelli as the appropriate topographical model for this third and final section of the *Comedy* in which Dante finally leaves all earthly spheres to be united with God (Altcappenberg 2000: 220–221).

At the centre of this cosmos was the earth. But that earth was the place of man's sins, punished eternally in Hell at earth's centre. It was the place where, through repentance during one's life, time spent in Purgatory (where the punishment for sin imposed by God is no less harrowing than it is in Hell) is not eternal. Souls in Purgatory can and do eventually progress from earth: to a Paradise far above it.

The idea of earth which rules this imaginary landscape is one in which, as in the Noah episode, our planet is merely the stage upon which God metes out punishment for sin and rewards for repentance. In Dante's scenario it functions conspicuously as the place where eternal life is to be earned and present life endured. As we shall see, Aristotelian cosmology played a role in this downgrading of earth itself. For in that cosmology, immobility was seen as a property of inert, corrupt matter (Blumenberg 1987: 138–139).

The geocentricity of the universe was not, therefore, an indication of *earth's* importance but of *man's* importance. In Dante's Christian cosmography, the most recalcitrant sinners are buried in a Hell placed at the centre of earth. Their punishment effectively is to remain on earth, or rather *in* earth, forever. This Christian version takes us from a Noah figure instrumental in saving a representative sample of all creatures, to a time when Christ earns Christians (alone) the power to repent and so avert punishment by God. We can, then, see it as courageous, if not audacious of Dante to make the pre-Christian Virgil his guide through Purgatory and Cato its guardian, even though he must leave them behind to ascend to the earthly Paradise under the guidance of his Christian love, Beatrice.

Botticelli includes recognizably beautiful earthly plants and flowers as living elements in the earthly Paradise, reflecting an interesting and rather ambivalent attitude towards earth. It was important not only as the place where man (literally) worked out his redemption but it was also potentially redeemable. Redeemable from what? From the conditions attached to its position in the universe. So the early Christian reformers taught (in continuity with what Dante had been taught) that as heaven epitomized a totally God-centred universe, life there could only be conceived of as being diametrically opposed to what constitutes life in an earth-centred universe. Anything else was literally unimaginable.

This is one reason why Luther merely made a dismissive remark about the possible heliocentric universe advocated by his contemporary Copernicus, while Calvin simply ignored it.[2] For Luther believed, as did his contemporaries, that the earth was the centre of a universe with exceedingly pure upper regions, but that as one moved downwards, the spheres became increasingly impure. But he and Calvin also believed in the sovereignty of God over all the universe, and argued that, at the end of time, like an alchemist who extracts and separates out the spirit, the life and the strength from the unclean matter that remains 'at the bottom' of earth, that is, in hell, God would finally purify the earth. So after the Last Judgement the earth (except for its hellish bowels) would be purified, renewed and refashioned. 'The flowers, leaves and grass will be as beautiful, pleasant and delightful as an emerald, and all creatures most beautiful.' Animals and plants would live for eternity in their newly perfected state. The blessed would not live there, although Luther thought that they might visit it. Calvin, however, did not think they would want to. Eternal life for them would mean existence in a God-centred universe: one centred on the eternal vision of God (McDannell 2001: 152–154).

In Chapter 6 I shall discuss in rather more detail this oppositional framework in which heaven is exalted and earth debased. It may well be true, as Dillenberger says, that the spatial connotations and the idea of Hell being at the centre of the earth became less important than how to avoid going there (Dillenberger 1988: 64). Nevertheless, such visualizations of our ideas about the earth, about ourselves and God's purposes for human life have become commonplace and have inclined us, no less than Dante, Botticelli, Luther and Calvin, to consider earth as no more than (hopefully) a staging post on the way to our real destiny, Paradise, and inclined us to the implicit belief that to reach that, we must, metaphorically at least, leave earth behind.

Ptolemaic cosmology

Such an identity of ourselves with a realm beyond the spheres was given a practical visual reference by the Ptolemaic cosmological system and this kind of Christian interpretation of it. Together they provided the religious imaginative frame of reference for Dante (as a representative educated Christian), just as they provided Botticelli with the necessary diagrams and the Roman Church with an apparently unshakeable conviction that it had the right to refute Copernicus and Galileo. This was, in no small part, because Ptolemy's diagrams were visibly acceptable (in contrast to those of Galileo), and empirically verifiable (in contrast to Copernicus). They displayed the commonly observed, and therefore common sense view of the paths of the sun, the moon and the known planets as well as the rotation of the sun and the planets around the earth.

This view held firm even though the Ptolemaic system had been setting insoluble problems for Renaissance astronomers who tried to apply mathematical principles to the movements of the stars. Indeed it was this 'lack of certitude in the traditional mathematics' that spurred Copernicus into carrying out his own mathematical researches into the Pythagorean philosophers and eventually discovering, as he said, 'that if the movements of the other wandering stars are correlated with the circular movement of the earth, and if the movements are computed in accordance with the revolution of each planet' (Copernicus 1992: 4–5), then greater mathematical symmetry is obtained. However, he had not solved all the problems. Definitive mathematical and visual evidence for his position had to wait for the work done by Kepler and Galileo, and it was only in 1687 that Newton's *Principia* finally brought into being a unified conception of the universe. Although this too had its problems, it made the basic Copernican position scientifically irrefutable (Dillenberger 1988: 25–28).

Ptolemy's authority remained practically unassailable for as long as it did because, as I said, the empirical evidence for his system accorded with those biblical passages which assumed the centrality of the earth and the movement of the sun, such as Psalms 19, 45, 69, 78, Proverbs 1:4, Ecclesiastes 1:5 and the passage about Joshua commanding the sun to stand still (Joshua 10:12–13). It also supported an Aristotelian as well as a Pythagorean or Platonic view of the universe, which held that the earth is at rest in the centre of the universe. All of which reinforced Ptolemy's cultural ascendancy. His *Geography* had been the standard treatise on that subject for over a thousand years. In it he linked his cosmology with his geography, stating that 'one must contemplate the extent of the entire earth, as well as its shape and its position under the heavens, in order that one may rightly state what are the peculiarities and proportions of the part with which one is dealing'. Columbus owned a Latin translation of this work made in 1479, and used Ptolemy's estimate of the size of the earth to argue for the feasibility of his proposed voyage of discovery. It gave him the confidence he needed to set sail for Asia, unfounded as it happens, as Ptolemy had underestimated the size of the earth, over-estimated that of Asia and had recorded no land mass between Asia and Europe (Osserman 1995: 20–24).

The 'revolution' of Copernicus's title called, therefore, for deep and ever-expanding revolutions within cultural and cosmic, geographical and theological imagination, as well as a revolution in self-perception. This was the case even though, for Copernicus himself, the '*revolutionibus*' only refers to an actual physical, spatial reality, that is, to the revolution or rotation of the planets around the sun. For him, and for later astronomers like Kepler and Galileo who accepted and endorsed his view, this was the primary revolution in every sense. But his hesitancy in publishing a description of it showed, as with Aristarchus, an awareness of its secondary revolutionary meanings. It involved nothing less than a turning away from a position generally held to be true and unchanging that was sanctioned by the religion, philosophy, science, custom and observation of the time. Above all, it meant a turn away from the central position in the universe given to man by God.

The Copernican revolution also involved a turning *towards* an unfamiliar, threatening and incalculable position: one in which the earth, the centre of *our* world, is no longer the centre of the universe. The closely knit and compact universe was gone and man was exposed, Dillenberger comments, to the dread of infinity in spatial terms. The comfortable, secure interrelation of space and destiny was threatened. And here lies the real cause for unease. It is our own position in the universe, our own centrality in the relationship between earth and heaven, between one heavenly body housing us and the heavenly bodies surrounding it, between ourselves on earth and God in heaven, that is seen to be at stake. Those who first read and reacted to Copernicus's work, and those who later reflected on its proven truth in Galileo's experiments and Kepler's calculations, perceived, however inchoately, that the real challenge is to the view that man (not his earth) holds, and is safely held in, the cosmic place of honour. And that God has put him there.

Theological anthropology

In Copernicus's day prevailing European cosmologies which assumed our holding the cosmic place of honour also assumed that it is our mind or soul or consciousness or reason within us which holds it. That is what places *homo*, man, at the centre of 'the heavens': at the centre of divine regard. The Christian doctrine supporting this homocentric view (one influenced by Plato, Aristotle and Augustine) held that the human soul or mind or consciousness, placed (by God) at the apex of creation, is at the same time the centre of God's relationship to the universe. Or, to be more precise, the human *male* soul or mind or consciousness or reason. Augustine wrote in *The Confessions* that:

> we see man, made in your [God's] image and likeness, ruling over all the irrational animals for the very reason that he was made in your image and resembles you, that is, because he has the power of reason and understanding.
>
> (Lloyd 1989: 111–128)

This doctrine of human supremacy, founded on man's rationality as an image of the divine, refers back directly to the dénouement of the Noah story and the sacrosanct nature of human life. But by Augustine's time there is an added twist to it. All other animals lack God's image, that is, they lack rationality. Human rationality is therefore both a sufficient and necessary cause for our ruling over them. The power of reason is equated with human power to control. Rationality, embodied in the male human form, is presumed to reign supreme over all 'irrational' forms of life, including women and children (Primavesi 2001b: 121–140).

By the time of Copernicus and Galileo there was another factor at play in this homocentrism. Teachings about Christ, the only Son of God, summed up in the credal statement *et homo factus est* (and was made man), had reached new levels of sophistication. The doctrine of human supremacy was reinforced by being essentially argued for on the basis of the centrality of Christ, central, that is, to human (Christian) history and to the history of the universe. He, the archetypal image of God, 'the first-born of all creation', the male representative human being, was seen as the symbolic centre of universal history. Human history itself was therefore seen as central to the history of the known universe. Christocentrism, homo-centrism and geocentrism mutually reinforced each other, especially as the history of Christ, humanity and the earth were practically conflated. (I shall go into this at some length in Chapter 3.) In the sixth century CE, Pope John I made the putative date for Christ's birth the central feature of the public Christian calendar, one in force to this day. Hence 'the' millennium celebrations.

Presupposed here in the claim made for the centrality of human reason or consciousness on earth, as for the centrality of human history within universal history, is the religious homocentric claim that man is at the centre of God's regard and therefore at the centre of the universe. And so all that there is, is there for us: there for us to control and to use for our purposes. This conclusion, whether religiously made or not, was and is the imputed authority and justification behind the monumental chemical, physical and biological changes in the earth's surface and biosphere brought about by us up to and throughout the twentieth century and continuing apace. And behind it also lies Aristotle's view of the earth as 'inert matter': there to be exploited in the vast construction and deconstruction projects of the past 200 years or so.

The claim that the earth is there 'for us' is common ground between thoroughgoing scientific secular humanism and orthodox Christianity. Science generally presupposes that rationality itself, or human 'intelligent information-processing', is sufficient cause for our being the controlling force on earth. Indeed the further claim is made (in an argument called the 'Anthropic Cosmological Principle' to be discussed in Chapter 2) that human rationality is sufficient cause for the evolution of the universe. Whatever form this scientific claim takes it has been, and is, gladly and gratefully accepted in a culture where science now holds the epistemologically privileged position once held by the Church. Scientists are now considered worthy and welcome champions against any present challenge to claims for our cosmic importance, particularly when, as is the case with Gaia theory, that challenge comes from within science. Behind their response, as we shall see, often lurks the presupposition that we are radically distinct from, rather than integrally bound to earth, or to Gaia.

Theologically the claims still presuppose and are supported by doctrines about human supremacy in which supremacy is conferred by God on a representative individual, Adam, or on other individuals, such as Noah, descended from him. Supreme among these, of course, is Christ. An important theological conclusion about him is that as he is God, then God chose to inhabit 'our' planet in distinction from all others. This (assumed) distinction marks it out, one might have thought, as peculiarly significant in its own right. However, as we shall see, that perception of earth was too much for the theologians and philosophers of Copernicus's day to take on board. Instead the emphasis remained solidly on us, and on the God revealed in Christ as 'one of us' and, by implication, not one of or with or for any other species. These exclusive and all-excluding claims seem to me not only arrogant about ourselves (or rather, about some of us), but supremely arrogant in regard to God. We, as it were, decide with whom, or how, or where God may be. Or not.

The claims not only disclose religious arrogance. They also point to an uncompleted turn in the cultural Copernican revolution which has, by default, had profound consequences for our perception of the earth's significance. Copernicus saw the universe, says Koyré, from the point of view of a mathematician and geometer. The geometrization of his thought was sufficiently strong and deep-seated to bring about a noticeable change in the Aristotelian concept of form. In regard to the motion of heavenly bodies, the Aristotelians had 'substantial form' in mind, that is, that the natural motion of the body in question is determined by the specific nature and definite substantial form of the body's matter. Copernicus, however, thought in terms of *geometrical* form, and in particular of the spherical shape of the celestial bodies. If they move, it is not because they possess a specific nature but simply because they are the most perfectly shaped to move.

This being so, Copernicus dealt at great length with the sphericity of the earth, a fact that was not in dispute in his time. He then used this to argue for the same circular motion being applicable to the earth as to the planets (Copernicus 1992: 9–12). This may seem blindingly obvious to us, but at the time the term 'celestial body' (planet) was not used of the earth. It was considered non-celestial, belonging to 'the sub-lunary world, the unworthy world and cesspool of corruption'. It was heavy, inert, motionless. Geometrization of the concept of form lifted the earth out of this state, placed it among the stars and raised it, so to speak, into the heavens. It is not sufficiently appreciated by us, says Koyré, that by placing the sun at the centre of the universe Copernicus returned to the Pythagorean position and completely overthrew the hierarchy of positions in the ancient and medieval cosmos.

There the central position was not the most honourable, but, on the contrary, the most unworthy. It was, in effect, the *lowest*, and consequently suited to the earth's imperfection. Perfection was located *above*, in the celestial vault above which again were 'the heavens' (Paradise), whilst 'Hell' was deservedly placed beneath the surface of earth (Koyré 1973: 59, 114f., n24; Primavesi 1991: 92–110). A glance back at what I said about Dante and Botticelli bears this out. It also bears out what I said at the beginning about the ambivalence of geocentricism. It can be used now, as it was then, to demonstrate not the value or dignity of the earth itself, but of our species as the one which lives on earth but is chosen out of it to be uniquely valued in the universe. Therefore in the Noah story, earth's own fate as well as that of the rest of its inhabitants hinges upon what we do. So Thomas Burnet attributed the 'deformity' of earth into mountains and valleys to Noah's flood, caused by man's sin (Gould 1987: 21–61). Earth's physical structure, it is assumed, is formed for us and deformed by us according to how we behave. We act, it is presupposed, as the mediators between God and the earth and our conduct is taken as the sole basis for any outcome of that mediation.

This religious presupposition is implicit in scientific arguments for human supremacy being based on our faculty of reason. Whichever form it takes, we know, scientifically, that precisely the opposite is true. Our fate is to be totally dependent on the earth for the essential resources needed to sustain our life. Ironically, we also know now that our immediate fate depends on our conduct in regard to those essential resources. And as they are being threatened more and more by our activities, a revolutionary turn in our relationship with the earth seems not only imperative but scientifically rational. Such a turn would be one which effectively reverses the role of our geocentrism, making it the focal point in our necessarily homocentric worldview. For we shall always see the earth from within our place there. Now we need to see that place in the light of earth's significance. Rational self-interest alone endorses that view because of the role the earth plays in our biological survival.

This form of geocentrism might also induce in us, or in some cases revive, a sense of awe at earth's capacity to sustain life over billions of years. And that might help counteract the religious/scientific premise about our being uniquely equipped with reason and so in control of all other creatures. Awareness of the pre-Copernican character of our geocentrism might also help us connect our ever more destructive activity to the perception we have of the earth as inert, corrupt, made of 'dirt'. In which case our refusal to see ourselves as being naturally part of, or made of, the same 'matter' is hardly surprising. If we view earth's 'substance' as being beneath us, in every sense, then understandably we might want to assume that we have been given an 'added-value' component (whether we call it soul, reason or mind) which sets us apart, potentially at least, from earthiness and corruption.

In its Christian version we call this component 'soul', and learn at an early age, as I did, that it is the soul which makes us like to God (Blumenberg 1987: 190). And also that it makes us unlike any other earthly creature. However it is argued for, it serves to reinforce our sense of the superiority of soul over body: the latter being unmistakably linked to every other life form on earth. Earth's low status is further stressed in the narratives about Christ's death (and, indeed, about that of his mother, Mary) where after death their bodies are carefully removed from contact with earth. (There is an echo here of Calvin's refusal to believe that people would want to resume contact with the earth.) His body ascends back 'up' into heaven: hers is taken up by angels. Botticelli shows us Dante and Beatrice following the same path and finding Christ and Mary 'up' there.

Such religious images have conspired to keep us in a pre-Copernican attitude towards the material body of earth. They have reinforced the assumption that it has no intrinsic value, no heavenly worth. That it is there to be used for our own ends. From a religious perspective, that end may be and is spoken of as eternal life in heaven. In our secularized culture it is usually imagined as economic gain and security. So as social theorist Nicholas Luhmann remarked, by consistent use of such coding as 'earthly' opposed to 'heavenly' and 'sacred' opposed to 'secular', the process of secularizing the earth which made its industrialized degradation possible followed on logically from the de-sacralizing of the earth within Christianity (Primavesi 2000: 67). In both cases, earth is seen as expendable in the achievement of human happiness, whether conceived of as heavenly or economic. And unlike Luther or Calvin, there is no concern shown for its future regeneration or rehabilitation.

In the final chapters of *Sacred Gaia* I looked at how this attitude has become entrenched in western society, especially in the very odd notion that the earth belongs to us (rather than the other way round). We say we own land and its resources, and sign documents of ownership for certain pieces of it. But how can we say we *own* something which was evolving for billions of years before we were born and will continue to do so after we are gone? However, this irrational and unfounded claim has allowed us to build up a very inflated sense of our own value, while deflating the earth's value. For ownership, after all, implies the power to use, to control, to dispose of something or to exploit its potential as best suits us. We assume possession of the earth, or some part of it, and are prepared to contest that claim; if necessary, even kill to support it. Then we feel free to use the land in whatever way pleases us and/or increases our status in the eyes of others. In western culture it is ultimately reduced to its commodity value, which, assessed solely as monetary 'assets', is used to enhance our own. The universalizing of this perception is evident in indignant international responses to China's claim to be on the point of colonizing the moon and utilizing its resources. The indignation relies on the assumption that 'the moon belongs to all of us'. Indeed.

So, long after Copernicus, we continue down the narrow homocentric path which practically ignores the earth because it is beneath us. Except, that is, when it comes to the question of who owns it and who can exploit its resources. This attitude of ownership, as Rilke saw, also has consequences for our attitude to others, and to God. For if, he says, we see the world like this we are likely to see them (and the moon) in the same way.

You must not worry, God.
They say: 'it's mine' of everything,
which suffers this in silence.
They're as wind which lightly strokes a branch and says: MY TREE...
They say: my life, my wife, my dog, my child,
yet know full well that everything: life, wife, dog and child
is but an alien image,
which blindly, with outstretched hands, they stumble on.
This truth is surely discerned only by those great enough
to long for eyes to see it.
Because the others REFUSE to learn that their paltry ramblings
create no bond with anything around them.
But, driven from possessions that they prize,
unrecognized by their own belongings
they OWN wives no more than they own flowers...
Dear God, hold on to your self-possession.
Even those who love you and discern your face in darkness,
like a flame trembling in your breath – do not possess you.

(Rilke 1975: 48. Trs. C. Carr and A. Primavesi)

2 After Copernicus

Chapter 1 mapped part of the cultural, religious and scientific landscape around Copernicus. It also indicated areas relatively untouched by the revolution initiated by him. In this chapter I want to take a closer look at some of the forces which kept that revolution within certain bounds.

Bertolt Brecht's play, *Life of Galileo*, is helpful here. In it, and in his reflections on the history of its writing, Brecht gives a voice to some passionately held negative reactions to Galileo and his role in furthering the Copernican revolution. Those reactions flowed naturally from a social and cultural consciousness in which authoritative patterns of interpretation, laid down by and reinforced through Christian teaching, almost guaranteed rejection of what Galileo said. By expressing that rejection dramatically, Brecht helps us once again to make an imaginative leap into a worldview so apparently different to ours. I say apparently, for, as we shall see, while we no longer say we believe that the earth is the centre of the universe, we have not moved much, if at all, from the then vehemently expressed corollary of that belief: that we are at its centre.

Brecht also helps us discern the role played, then and now, by the relative epistemological privilege accorded to religion and science. Both exercise this privilege, now as then, within a social process where the knowledge of one person counts for more than that of another. And the privileged status of one over the other affects society in many different ways, not least in its reception of new knowledge. The Church's knowledge counted in Galileo's time to such an extent as to ensure the rejection of his scientific discoveries. Now scientific knowledge counts significantly for more in western culture and generally ensures acceptance of scientific interpretations of most phenomena even when, and at times especially when, this means rejecting the claims of religion.

Brecht wrote the initial draft of *Life of Galileo* in 1938, after he had fled Nazi Germany. The final version of 1945 was based on a revision done with Charles Laughton after the Second World War. I first read the play, and still do, as a dramatic account of the relative force behind a new idea about our-selves compared with that currently accepted in society, and of how the strength of the latter may be sufficient for the knowledge behind the new idea to be totally rejected. For knowledge does not exist in a personal or social vacuum. At the time in which the play is set, the knowledge that we live in a heliocentric rather than a homocentric universe was rejected because it implied an idea of ourselves which was reckoned, in religious terms, to be wholly objectionable. The objections to it (that is, to its poten-tial de-centring of man) are brilliantly conveyed in a dramatic outburst from a character called 'The Very Old Cardinal'. He denounces Galileo as 'an enemy of the human race': inimical, that is, to a view of ourselves as 'the crown of creation'. His antagonism towards Galileo and his total rejection of Copernican theory come from what he sees as their deadly threat to this idea of himself. To lose it would mean, for him, losing all significance (including that of earth) before God and in the eyes of men. For those he represents, then and now, earth's significance radiates out from man as its centre:

> I am not any old creature on any insignificant star briefly circling in no particular place. I am walking with a firm step, on a fixed earth; it is motionless, it is the centre of the universe. I am at the centre and the eye of the Creator falls on me and on me alone.
>
> (Brecht 1980: 54)

The cardinal insists that the mighty sun has been created to illuminate his surroundings, and to illuminate him too, so that God may see him. The car-dinal goes on to insist: 'In this way, everything comes visibly and incontro-vertibly to depend on me, mankind, God's great effort, the creature on whom it all centres, made in God's own image.' This is about as clear a statement of anti-Copernicanism as one can find. It is also, of course, a powerful summary of the religious argument for human supremacy. In these less overtly religious times, his attitude to Galileo expresses the gener-ally held and contemporary view that anyone who opposes homocentrism is misanthropic. To claim significance for forms of life other than the human is routinely dismissed as evidence of hatred for our own species.

Brecht, however, first saw the play in terms of a common problem for himself and for Galileo: the problem of how to respond to political oppres-sion. Galileo experienced oppression in seventeenth-century Italy where the Inquisition reigned supreme; Brecht in twentieth-century Germany with Hitler supreme. Brecht was also exercised about the crucial relationship between science and authoritarian regimes, especially the role scientists play within them. In this regard he first saw Galileo's silence (or rather more properly, silencing) playing a relatively innocent role, in that it passively supported (when it could have undermined) the authority of the Church and the ruling classes. Brecht realized that the power latent in scientific knowledge can be used either to liberate others or to support their oppression. For there is always an inextricable link between the exercise of knowledge and the exercise of power: between the privilege knowledge bestows on those who hold it within societies and communities and their use of that epistemological privilege to favour their own interests or to further their own ends.

Galileo's knowledge was privileged above that of the peasants, but not above that of the Church. And the Church's exercise of privilege included, as it so often did then, direct physical power over his body. Challenging that privilege was, in effect, challenging its presupposition, that is, that its knowledge was given to the Church by God. That was then enough (for those inside the Church) to justify the threat of torture. They were, they claimed, acting in God's name. And perhaps one could say that Galileo had internalized that justification to the extent that, in conjunction with his isolation as an individual before the corporate power of the Church, and his physical frailty, it made it easier for him to recant. If so (and I shall return to this) it makes his recantation even more understandable. But it does not make this use of the Church's privilege any more acceptable. In fact, for me it makes it worse. The use and abuse of epistemological privilege takes many forms, but the most theologically sinister is using it to justify violence in God's name.

However, when Brecht later collaborated with Charles Laughton on an English translation and revision of the text, the detonation of the atom bomb at Hiroshima changed the moral of the play for him. He now saw science in general playing an active and decisive role in the Second World War, a perception subsequently strengthened by the Cold War and the development of the hydrogen bomb. Initially he had set Galileo within a world where the Church functions as an authority with a vested interest in the status quo, in that any questioning of the religious framework which kept the peasants docile, even if not contented, would affect the privileges of the Church just as much as those of the landowners. In such a world Brecht originally attributed a vision to Galileo in which science could, if it had the courage and the desire, lighten the common man's burden through an empirical, rationalist and materialist strand of thinking bound up with progressive social theories. Now, however, he saw the figure of Galileo as subservient to the ruling classes, a subservience Brecht saw as a crime which led in a direct line to the abuse of science by the Nazis, with the abuse being compounded by the complicity of scientists in the abuse and subservience of others. So in the final version of the play, the moral is for the scientist: stand up and be counted! After Hiroshima, Brecht felt that the scientist could not evade moral responsibility for the use to which his work was put (Brecht 1980: xxi–xxv, 53–54). 'The atomic bomb, both as a technical and social phenomenon, is the classical end product of scientific accomplishment and its failure' (Oberman 1986: 183, quoting Brecht). The failure is, of course, to safeguard the life and liberty of those not privileged – by knowledge, class, background or circumstance.

The role of knowledge

I have gone into the background and development of Brecht's play at some length in order to underline the ambivalent role of knowledge, whether religious or scientific, before, during and since the original Copernican revolution. Whether religious or scientific, its possession and use by those in power affects society as a whole. It does so in two ways. First by imposing policies justified on the basis of privileged knowledge, and second, by using the weight of privilege to determine what kind of knowledge is endorsed by public policy and becomes socially effective. In Galileo's case, the silence imposed on him and on what he knew was justified by weighing it against the knowledge attributed to the Church. The weight of this was enough to discredit his knowledge and make it unacceptable for others to agree with him.

The demarcation lines between the power of different kinds of knowledge is not so clear now as it was then. And even then, as we shall see in Chapter 3, there were forces outside the Church's control which contributed eventually to the acceptance of Galileo's evidence for a heliocentric universe. Today the response to new theories is more disparate and diffused. But the point Brecht is making, as I understand it, is that the scientific knowledge of the atomic weapon scientists, allied as it was to political and/or military power, was privileged to an extent which made the use to which that knowledge was put generally acceptable to society. That is, to the society in which the western allies (excluding Russia) lived. But it would not have made it acceptable to the Japanese society which was going to suffer its effects: nor to a small band of scientists sympathetically aware of those who might suffer them in future.

We have moved here from a period in which the effects of epistemological privilege (then held by the Church) were more or less limited by geographical boundaries to one in which, for a variety of reasons, different kinds of knowledge inevitably have comprehensive and incalculable effects on society and on the earth as a whole. Scientists, Brecht thought, have to take responsibility for them. He exposes a prevailing fallacy about scientific knowledge: that there is a sort of abstract information available only to scientists which can be held impartially by them (such as splitting the atom, or mapping the human genome) without their having to take account of its effects on the lives of others or on the resource base of life on the planet. One of my aims in this book is to expose this fallacy in the religious realm. Christians cannot go on thinking that they *know* that God has made them the centre of the universe without taking account of the effects of this idea on the whole household of life on earth.

The fallacy is most clearly exposed however, because most baldly stated, in the realm of scientific knowledge. There it is supposed and claimed that this form of knowledge can and should be divorced from any emotion-laden content or interpretation. And, that it can be used without taking responsibility for how its results may affect people's lives. This supposes, in other words, that human knowledge of a particular kind exists in a bodily and emotional vacuum – as do those who possess it or those who use it. Mary Midgley quotes some relevant statements to this effect, such as Professor Ernest Chain's declaration that 'no quality of good or evil is attached to results of research', or 'can be ascribed to' them. She goes on to discuss the kind of autonomy attributed to scientific knowledge under the heading 'The Seclusion of Science'. She notes, for a start, that autonomy, which began as a political concept, never presupposed isolation from a larger body politic.

Then she goes on to give a rough guide to the presuppositions, usually unspoken, which lie behind this presumed seclusion of science from society. It is supposed, for instance, that scientists are always guided by the evidence and never by their wishes. Then, that purely factual propositions can never have practical or evaluative consequences. Therefore, when selecting subjects for enquiry, it is supposed that scientists are guided only by relevance, never by outside pressures or by concern for the good or harm that will result from their enquiries. She makes another very pertinent point in regard to contemporary scientific autonomy. Scientists need not, it is assumed, concern themselves about the conditions which make their enquiries possible, nor are they responsible for anything objectionable about the sources of their funds, even when this is known to them (Midgley 1989: 74–88).

Brecht's discernment of the deprivileging of scientific knowledge relative to the overprivileged knowledge of the Church at the time of Galileo brings into sharp relief how those roles are now reversed. His insight into the relationship between science and the ways in which it serves (or not) the ideology of the ruling classes was deepened, of course, by his own experience of the unaccountable power exercised by a regime whose ideology was endorsed and literally 'executed' by science. In Galileo's ideoscape of seventeenth-century Italy, Roman Catholic ideology relied on the common acceptance of the God-given authority of (some in) the Church who used that authority to impose that view of themselves. In twentieth-century Germany, this mutually sustaining interaction was upheld by Nazi theories of racial supremacy enforced by armed power and the collusion of science. It too centred on the centrality of *some* of humankind, those of Aryan descent. In both cases, however, the basic premise of the absolute significance and privileging of the knowledge of (some of) humankind, which worked to their own advantage, held sway. And it was the execution of that power over other human beings which outraged Brecht.

Scientific privilege

Similar executions of power over others continue to outrage me and many others. But today we would want to extend that outrage to the unaccountable execution of human power, by executives of many types, over 'the beasts of the field, the creeping things and the birds of the air'. We would also want to question the assumptions behind that executive power which, in practical respects, has changed little since the time of Noah. Except, of course, that its biblical authority is seldom invoked. The presupposition now (as we saw in the preceding chapter) is that human rationality, or 'intelligent information processing', gives science, or at least certain types of science, publicly privileged power over all non-human forms of life.

One relevant instance is the way in which the 2001 outbreak of foot-and-mouth disease in Britain was handled. The power of the army, the civil service, the police and the ministry of agriculture (MAFF) was deployed in a mass slaughter policy which allowed no appeals. One woman who tried to save her five pet pedigree sheep from preventive slaughter (there was no evidence they were infected) had her home invaded by MAFF officials supported by Gurkha soldiers and police. The overriding consideration was the decision of the 'chief scientist' to slaughter all animals on land contiguous to infected herds, with the aim of restoring trading status to Britain's meat exporters. Human economic considerations alone were taken into account and between four and six million 'unclean' animals, at least one-third of them disease-free, were sacrificed to the great God Mammon: to the Market. For it has been established that the option of vaccination was first decided on and then abandoned by the government at the behest of multinational corporations and some farmers fearful for their overseas markets.

After five months of this slaughter, when the disease still appeared active and some sheep tested positive for antibodies, the logic behind the policy degenerated into this: if animals have had the disease (i.e. developed antibodies) and recovered: kill them. If they have it now: kill them. If they are likely to get it: kill them. If they have not had it and are not likely to get it (but cannot be exported): kill them (Letter to the *Guardian*: August 6, 2001). This 'policy' was proposed by government ministers, on scientific advice, and implemented as a rational, non-emotive response to the outbreak.

Where then, is the challenge to human supremacy, or rather the assumption of that supremacy, to come from today? One possible wake-up call, as I said in the Introduction, may come from our increasing knowledge of the effects of that supremacy. To date, however, this has proved an inadequate challenge to the idea of ourselves as uniquely privileged by our rationality. It has also proved woefully inadequate in challenging the idea of ourselves as owners of the earth and of its resources: there for us to exploit and use for our own ends. Within the Christian establishment where so many of the presuppositions behind human supremacy shelter (and are adopted in secularized form by those who ignore or are ignorant of its history), the task has scarcely begun. For here it is presumed that the ultimate epistemological privilege belongs to God, who has 'spoken through Moses and the prophets and finally, through his Son, Jesus Christ'. And what has he said? As I routinely discover, it is taken to be something that echoes uncannily what was said by Brecht's cardinal.

When asked to speak to a Roman Catholic group on the issues raised by *Sacred Gaia*, I decided to summarize the issues in the light of what I have been saying here about the Copernican revolution. The session started with a meditation prepared by the group in which some prayers actually included the phrase 'we are the crown of creation': repeating, that is, almost verbatim, the cardinal's speech. But that was scarcely surprising. In 1964, twenty years after Brecht wrote it, cardinals in Rome at the Second Vatican Council proclaimed that 'all things on earth should be related to man [sic] as their centre and crown ... having been created in the image of God ... man [sic] was appointed by Him [sic] as master of all earthly creatures that he might subdue them and use them to God's glory ... [for] man [sic] is *the only creature on earth which God willed for itself* (Abbott 1966: 210f., 223. My italics).

The breath-taking arrogance of that final sentence is, of course, a claim to our having been specially created by God outside the normal course of evolution. It echoes Brecht's cardinal's view of us as 'God's great effort'. As I quoted him and then went on to contrast this view with the reality of our belonging firmly within the shared evolutionary history of life on earth I glimpsed a look of consternation on the face of the person responsible for the meditation. At the same time I glimpsed the continuing revolutionary character within Christianity of Copernicus's question about our place in the universe, and within the earth community. In a public lecture series organized by a cathedral, when I quoted Brecht and expanded on the cardinal's outburst, I was challenged by a scientist who said she agreed with all I said about our interdependence with all living beings, but in the end, we have unique status within creation 'because we alone have souls'. This, she inferred, makes humans exceptional.

Outside of traditional Christian hierarchies, science now appears to rely on, and at the same time to appeal to, a rather different presupposition for human epistemological privilege and our right to use it no matter what its effects. I say 'appears to', because behind it lies the same sort of isolationist idea about ourselves (although not about God) as that held by the Catholic Church when it rejected Galileo and restated by it today. Scientific epistemological privilege adduces a particular idea of human rationality, evident in our ability to compute, to argue for the centrality of that rationality within the universe. To the point where an *assumption* about the centrality of human rationality becomes a conclusion about the purpose behind the universe.

The Anthropic Principle

In a major book entitled *The Anthropic Cosmological Principle,* the authors John Barrow, a distinguished astronomer, and Frank Tipler, a similarly distinguished professor of mathematics and physics, offer a collection of ideas as 'a means of relating Mind [sic] and observership directly to the phenomena traditionally within the compass of physical science'. The word *anthropic* here has the same function as *homo*, that is, one may assume that it is intended to refer to the whole human race. So the title suggests that the existence of our species constitutes a principle in relation to the existence of the entire universe.

The principle itself connects 'Mind' (human) and our capacity to observe and understand what happens in the world with our unique status (observership). This principle is then taken as fundamental to the evolution of the universe. In other words, our rational, scientific capacity to observe and compute that evolution is taken as its goal and purpose. The destiny of the universe coincides with ours: which is to have 'minds' uniquely capable of observing it. The term 'observer' denotes an attitude of scientific non-attachment to what is being observed, so there is an implicit assumption that our 'observership' extends to and operates anywhere within the Universe. Geocentrism no longer limits our horizons. True, astronauts appear to support this assumption, but a moment's reflection reminds us that they bring with them the earthly atmosphere and physical resources their bodies need. They cannot (yet) live outside their terrestrial environment.

Barrow and Tipler say that they regard as axiomatic the Copernican principle which holds that we do not occupy a privileged position in the Universe. However they also say that 'like most generalizations [sic] it must be used with care' (1986: 1f.). Having thus carefully prepared the ground, they build the following conclusion on it: 'Although we do not regard our position in the Universe to be central or special in every way, this does not mean that it cannot be special in *any* way.' (ibid.) They go on to single out 'Mind and observership' as making the significant difference in respect to our position and cite our ability to compute the size of the Universe as displaying an intrinsic bias towards our evolution as 'minds' capable of observing and computing it. This argument for our significant difference takes exactly the same form as that used by theologians, although the latter cite our possession of a soul as making us special.[3]

They do not, however (as far as I know) go on to cite the soul's computing abilities as proof of their argument. Instead they base their claim on the human soul being like to God and therefore unlike any other creature on earth. Barrow and Tipler, however, have no referent outside ourselves to appeal to. This makes their argument a circular one, for they hypothesize 'Mind' of a particular sort as special to us and then use this 'Mind' to make us special within the Universe. Because, that is, we have worked out, through our minds, a satisfactory hypothesis about the size of the Universe. Satisfactory, that is, to our minds. How the Universe itself measures up to it remains unknown.

But the concept of 'Mind' is notoriously slippery, having at various times been taken as equivalent to soul, reason or rationality. So a theologian would, if so minded, be entitled to complete the theological circle of proof by saying that the human soul is uniquely capable of computing the size of the Universe because it is like to God. And on any usual definition of God, God alone knows its size because God made it the size it is. Or may be.

But no amount of scientific epistemological privilege can establish a claim to human omniscience in regard to the size or nature of the universe. Science by its very nature progresses through the discovery of new information that in some way or other calls for revision of conclusions whose inadequacy led to the new discovery, as happened with Copernicus. Nor do I think that Barrow and Tipler are staking a claim to omniscience. My concern here is not with the semantics of their argument but with the fact that it effectively neutralizes the challenge of the Copernican principle by transposing homocentrism (or more precisely human mind-centredness) into a principle of purpose in the universe. By doing so, our essential geo-centrism, that is, earthly body-centredness, is ignored if not implicitly denied.

So in spite of 'a general belief that teleology is scientifically bankrupt', Barrow and Tipler propose this particular twentieth-century form of homo-centrism as a principle of purpose. They then hedge their bets slightly by proposing a distinction between 'weak' and 'strong' versions of the anthropic principle. The former is defined as the requirement that the observed values of all physical and cosmological quantities are restricted by there being sites where carbon-based life can evolve and by the Universe being old enough for it to have already done so. The strong version simply states that 'the Universe *must* have those properties which allow life to develop within it at some stage in its history', or, that 'observers are *necessary* to bring the Universe into being' (my italics). Together these lead to the 'Final Anthropic Principle': that 'intelligent information-processing *must* come into existence in the Universe, and, once it comes into existence, it will never [sic] die out' (Barrow and Tipler 1986: 1–16, 21–23. My italics).

The smart move here is from 'life' (found in everything from viruses to trees to elephants) to 'intelligent information-processing': that is, to us, rationally privileged, usually male, scientifically literate humans. And while Barrow and Tipler go on to warn their readers that this is 'quite speculative and unquestionably not to be regarded as a well-established principle of physics', few will heed, or want to heed, their warning. For they themselves embody the privilege and power of scientific authority acceptable today to non-Christians and Christians alike. Not least because their proposal apparently liberates us from the uncomfortable feeling that perhaps the universe has purposes and aims *other* than ours. Or that in fact, *pace* current agribusiness policies, we are not the most significant form of life on earth with rights of possession over all the others.

Against anthropism

Barrow and Tipler are using a scientific version of a theological homocentric design argument, in which they themselves do not (although others may) proceed to name the 'Designer'. They do, however, quote Galileo on the subject of homocentric design. Or rather, on the kind of designer God implied by this. We arrogate too much to ourselves, Galileo said, 'if we suppose that the care of us is the adequate work of God, an end beyond which the divine wisdom and power does not extend'. In contrast to Kepler, who was quite happy to think that 'all things have been made for man', Galileo felt that such ideas were simply unthinking manifestations of human presumption (Barrow and Tipler 1986: 50). A God whose regard focuses solely on us appears to have no regard for the rest of the universe. Descartes, his contemporary, voiced precisely the same doubts. We ought to beware, he said, lest, in our presumption, we imagine that the ends which God proposed to himself in the creation of the world are understood by us (Descartes 1912: 212).

This theology, one could say, exhibits post Copernican humility. It presents evidence of the greatness of the universe but stays within the limits of that evidence in what it says about the purpose of the universe. Someone who, like Galileo, had for the first time on earth seen the moons of Jupiter, felt as the Psalmist did some two thousand years earlier when he looked at the night sky and exclaimed in wonder: 'When I look at the heavens and consider the works of your hands, who is man, O God, that you are mindful of him?' Galileo did not, however, on the evidence here, make the mistake of claiming that: 'You have delivered all things into his hands and put all things under his feet' (Psalm 8).

With the anthropic principle however, we find scientists in the curious position of supporting a theological worldview which Copernicus, on their own admission, would not have supported; one which Galileo and Descartes pronounced theologically suspect and Brecht exposed dramatically as plain hubris. In her analysis of Barrow and Tipler's language and logic Mary Midgley makes clear that the claims to privileged knowledge once based on the supposed access of ecclesiastics to 'the mind of God' are now, in the court of human appeal, routinely granted to science (and in this case appropriated by it) (Midgley 1992: 27–31, 195–209). Anthropologist Stewart Guthrie sums up: 'At best, anthropism appears an uneasy union of anthropocentrism and anthropomorphism, elevated to a principle' (Guthrie 1993: 169f.).

I want to go back here to Brecht's point about taking responsibility for the effects of scientific knowledge. What are the likely effects of Barrow and Tipler's elegant argument for human supremacy in the universe? Central to it is the assumption that we are capable of observing the evolving, expanding universe in its entirety and then reaching the conclusion that our existence is the aim and purpose of the entire process. A moment's reflection on this assumption shows the quite breathtaking arrogance behind it. It is arrogant in its presumption that we are capable of the breadth of knowledge and understanding required to observe the whole universe. It is arrogant in supposing that having achieved this humanly impossible feat, we can conclude, on its basis, that the universe evolved in order that we might do so. A second-order assumption follows: that we possess the breadth of knowledge and understanding required to observe the evolving earth in its entirety and draw unfailingly correct conclusions about its nature, operations and purpose, and about our role in them.

This arrogance has not, of course, gone unnoticed by scientists. The anthropic principle was first proposed in the 1970s by astrophysicist Brandon Carter, who then published it in 1983. He based it on assumptions about the average timescale for the evolution of intelligent life on planets (determined by biochemical reactions and evolution of species) and for the lifetime of a star (determined by nuclear reactions). Mario Livio, head of the science programme for the Hubble Space Telescope, deals with the scientific and mathematical aspects of Carter's argument. Having been bothered by this principle since Carter first formulated it, by 1998 Livio finally discovered a potential flaw in it. It lies in the assumption that the timescale for biological evolution and stellar evolution are independent quantities. Livio goes on to explain what this means in terms of ultraviolet radiation, surface temperatures on stars and the release of oxygen.

As a non-scientist, I cannot grasp the scientific complexities of his argument any more than those of Carter's original proposal. Nor do I want to misrepresent Livio, who says that 'it is important to emphasize that I cannot *prove* that Carter's argument is wrong, but I showed that it *could* be wrong'. What I can understand is the reason Livio gives for being 'extremely bothered by it'. Using Barrow and Tipler's formulations of the strong and weak versions of the principle, he says that while the argument behind it does not specifically *require* us to be special, 'its consequences, if true, would make us incredibly special'. This would, he admits, appeal to many. But to him 'it "smells" anti-Copernican' (Livio 2000: 243–250).

The idea of ourselves as 'incredibly special' is then, for Livio, anti-Copernican. As I shall argue later (pp. 65–68), Copernicus did not, in fact, greatly outrage the naïve self-love dramatically and clearly expressed in the cardinal's speech. It was, if anything, enhanced by the move to heliocentrism. Its characteristic expression, however, has changed to a scientific one. Its re-emergence in the anthropic principle shows how deeply rooted this idea has remained. It emerges accompanied by a scientific view of ourselves as 'observers': as being impartial in regard to, as well as physically detached from, whatever is being observed. 'Observer status' at the United Nations has all these resonances. At the psychological level the anthropic principle carries a significant 'feel-good' factor about ourselves, our capabilities and our place in the universe. Unfortunately it does so by setting us apart from all those other life forms which share our actual place there, and giving us the role of observers sanctions a certain attitude to those others.

This is an attitude (as Brecht learned and Midgley explained) to which science is particularly prone. It would like to believe that it has no responsibility for the effects of its research on society or, in this instance, for the effects on us of the image of ourselves as disinterested observers. The anthropic principle authorizes (in the sense of giving authority to) this image, one all the more acceptable for its resonance with that drawn earlier and again today by Christian cardinals. The scientific image, however, effectively substitutes our eyes for those of God. But with no benevolent gaze. For our relationship to the rest of the earth community is reduced to that of minds without bodies. This reductionism, so evident in the foot-

and-mouth crisis, effectively excludes all feelings of compassion, of love, of empathy and of shared joy from our relationships with other creatures. It appeals, in every sense, to the perception of science Mary Midgley brings to our attention: as being divorced by nature from all ethical and moral concerns.

Sir Ernest Chain's 1970s statement of this position (quoted on page 29) was presented as a declaration on the social responsibility of the scientist. Actually, it disclaimed all responsibility. Its doctrine of non-involvement has been well taught and learned, and regularly surfaces, and is appealed to, as an accepted part of scientists' self-perception. In July 2001, Joji Morishita, deputy director in the Far Seas Division of Japan's Fisheries Agency, defended its scientific research programme on whaling against objections to it by members of the international scientific community. They stated that 'moral and ethical issues are raised when a single research program results in more than 2,500 cetaceans being killed over eight years, with whale meat and other products resulting from such research being sold in commercial markets while a moratorium on commercial whaling remains in force'. His response to them was that their statement 'merely confirms that their concerns are ethical and moral *and [therefore] not scientific* (*The Ecologist*, 31, 6: 21. My italics). This argument presupposes that scientific research operates in a moral-free zone and has no regard, as Brecht saw, for the effects on others of what is done with its 'products', whether by governments or individuals.

Today the shift of privilege to science means that when scientists deprivilege all forms of life other than the human, all too often this deprivileging becomes normative within a culture. It also means that scientific knowledge which excludes itself from moral and ethical concerns, or which refuses to take account of its effects on the moral and ethical framework of society, must 'stand up and be counted!' And if this is true of those who have this knowledge and use it, then it is also true of those of us who, in varying degrees, grant it its privilege and assent to its use.

In *Sacred Gaia* I gave the example of how primary categories of Darwinian description, such as struggle, competition and 'the survival of the fittest' have become normative in sociobiological descriptions of human interaction (Primavesi 2000: 54f.). The repetition of such slogans affects our immediate reactions, which in turn affect our behaviour. We need to monitor their use, just as Christians today have to monitor the effects of religious slogans such as 'outside the church there is no salvation'. Scientists would be the first to dismiss this as an inhuman attitude to others. But they should also be concerned about inhuman responses to all sentient beings apparently sanctioned by science.

In the epoch from Copernicus to Hubble, scientific astronomy has raised many questions about our place in the universe, but the contemporary emergence and acceptance of the anthropic principle demonstrates that some answers true to Copernican science were and are still too painful and threatening to be generally accepted. Nietszche may have been right personally when he said that, for him, because of what he called the degrading and humiliating progress from Copernicus to Darwin, 'my importance is annihilated' (von Cues 1957: 7f.). But as Brecht learned painfully in the century after Nietzsche, and Livio now attests, history tells a rather different story. Or rather, with some updating, one much the same as that told about Noah.

3 Theological challenges to Copernicus

I want now to highlight some significant features of the Church's supremacy in Galileo's time that hindered the progress of the astronomical Copernican revolution. At the same time, as we shall see, events occurred outside its direct control, such as his experiments, new geographical and archaeological discoveries and the growth of literacy that led eventually to its completion.

One prominent feature of the Church's supremacy then was the fact that, in sharp contrast to today, a clear and unambiguous divide simply did not exist between what the scientist did and said in his professional life and what he believed (or not) about God. This, as I said already, made Galileo's scientific challenge even more difficult and more courageous than it might now appear. In varying degrees the same sort of courage was shown by his predecessor, Copernicus, and, as we shall see in this chapter, by his near contemporaries, Johann Kepler and Isaac de La Peyrère. All were Christians, the last named, it is true, ready to declare allegiance to Calvinism or to Roman Catholicism depending on circumstances. In his case, for very practical reasons of personal safety, he, too, like the others, considered himself bound to respect and indeed uphold Christianity's claims to privileged access in regard to knowledge of God.

This meant that they all embodied both the challenge of science to the biblical–Aristotelian–Ptolemaic picture of the world and resistance to that challenge. For, in varying degrees, they believed that the Church's knowledge is divinely inspired, that is, that God revealed it to men who transmitted it to others, including themselves, through an unbroken ecclesiastical tradition. As we have already seen, Augustine drew on the revelatory status and resultant authority of the Genesis account when he argued for man being made in the image of divine reason. And who relied more than the men in question on the power of reason to reach their scientific conclusions? So the experience of trying to privilege their own access to scientific knowledge while acknowledging the claims of publicly privileged ecclesiastical knowledge affected their responses to the latter. Some of these responses are still instructive for those of us who, at some time and in some fashion or other, find cherished inherited beliefs clashing with hard-won fresh insights or discoveries.

A major difference between then and now, however, is that the cultural context of sixteenth- and seventeenth-century Europe was one in which universal human history was practically equated with the history of Christ, and the Bible was read as a witness to Christ. Christocentrism based on the New Testament dictated that the history of the Jewish people, as recounted in the Jewish Scriptures, was treated as a preface to that of Christ. The genealogy in Luke's Gospel establishes Jesus as descended from 'Shem, the son of Noah, the son of Lamech, the son of Methuselah, the son of Enoch, the son of Jared, the son of Mahalale-el, the son of Ca-inan, the son of Enos, the son of Seth, the son of Adam, the son of God' (Luke 3:23–38).

Christian chronology

The formal public assimilation of Jewish history into Roman and then Christian history dates from the sixth century CE when Pope John I asked a monk, Dionysius Exiguus, to draw up a public calendar based on Christian chronology. Following the practice of the day, Dionysius dated events from the foundation of Rome (*ab urbe condita*), fixing the birth of Jesus (Christ) as 25 December 753 AUC. A further important step, taken in 1650, was the conflation of (Christian) human history with the history of the earth. A noted biblical scholar, Archbishop Ussher, took Dionysius's calendar as a reliable guide for calculating the chronology of the earth itself, dating its creation (and with it, that of Adam) in −4004, on 23 October, at noon. The end of the world would therefore happen on 23 October 1997, at noon, that is, exactly 2,000 years after the birth of Christ and 6,000 years after the creation of the world (Gould 2000: 8–13).

This biblical chronology, centred on the birth of Christ, is still accepted today by many Christians as literally true. In February 2000 a Gallup poll in America found that 45 per cent of Americans believed that God created humans in their present form within the past 10,000 years (reported in *Science and Spirit*, May/June 2001: 11). Even for those who do not accept this as literally true or bother about its basis, the timespan from 'Adam' to Christ to the end of the world is still often assumed to mark the beginning, middle and end of human history. In western Christian culture, Christ was and still is the pivotal figure, the midpoint of the timespan, referring back to its beginning, the creation of Adam, and forward to its end, when Christ returns in judgement. The birth of Jesus continues to be a fixed point. As does the creation of 'Adam'. This is so, even though the generally accepted geological timescale for the life of our planet is about 4,600 million years; for the emergence of life forms about 4,000–3,500 million years and for the emergence of hominids, our immediate ancestors, some hundreds of thousands of years.

In *The Christian Gene* I discussed some of the theological reasons for the retention of biblical chronology, or to be more precise, the enduring power of a theological doctrine of salvation neatly fitted within its timeframe (Primavesi 2001a: 3–8). The doctrine is fashioned out of interlocking elements or complementary concepts which follow the rules by which bi-polar pairs, such as Adam and Christ, sin and salvation, death and life, dovetail consistently within a narrative sequence that combines and recombines them, but always in ways that show salvation, Christ and life belonging together as do their polar opposites: sin, Adam and death. The essential opposition between an individual, Christ, and his mirror image, Adam, creates the interaction from which salvation flows. Adam's unique creation by God, and his sin, are the fixed points of reference for establishing the centrality of Christ in human salvation.

There is an interesting difference between this and the story of Noah. There God brings death on every living creature because of men's sins, and then not only saves some of them because Noah is righteous but promises not to curse earth again because humans sin. By contrast, the Adam–Christ relationship as traditionally expounded in Christianity commonly reserves the possibility of salvation from death to humans alone. Thoroughgoing Christian homocentrism takes no account, and gives no account to God, of the salvation of other living beings.

Going back to the seventeenth century, another reason why Ussher's biblical chronology (although not his dates) is still used as an accepted framework for human history is that, as church historian Klaus Scholder points out, the elements which go to form this ecclesiastically theological historical picture agreed, until about 400 years ago, with those of the physical picture of the universe accepted by every European and, by extension, in every European colony. I have a beautiful print on my wall of a twelfth-century tapestry of the creation of the world in which there is a large circle made up of segments depicting the various 'days' and types of creature described in the Genesis text. Inset is an inner circle where Christ sits at the centre of creation. In the slightly later geographical Mappa Mundi of Hereford, the known continents of Europe, Africa and Asia, surrounded by their seas, surround Jerusalem, while Christ reigns supreme over all. The prevalence and acceptance of this global picture, set against the background of Ptolemaic theological astronomy, was sufficient, right up to the time of Darwin, to resist the Copernican challenge to our being the most essential, the most loved and the most God-like beings in the universe. Noah, you remember, was given power over every living being on earth because, like Adam, he was made in God's image. In Christianity that image, scarred through Adam's sin, was fully restored through Christ. And with it the claim to absolute power over all creation.

One major difference between Copernican times and ours is, of course, that while 45 per cent of Americans may now believe that Adam was specially created by God, 400 years ago practically everyone in Europe, including Jews and Muslims, believed it. The majority of Europeans (including Copernicus, Kepler and Galileo) read Scripture as a textbook of incomparable status and unique quality, one older, more complete and more accurate than any other source. Scripture, church and world history formed a unified picture. And one with such power and coherence, on which so much of the reality of faith and human experience depends, does not fade out of consciousness overnight (Scholder 1990: 70–72).

In fact, says Scholder, in the period between 1550 and 1650, there are only intermittent signs that the critical questions which heralded the slow re-structuring of historical, personal and political consciousness were beginning to be formulated. They arose gradually under the influence of realities external to the traditional Christian framework, such as the growing geographical extension of perspectives beyond the limits of Western Europe. Columbus and other voyagers such as Magellan and Tasman brought home, literally and figuratively, new and undeniable historical realities to be pored over and analysed by an increasingly literate laity. Indeed, remarks Scholder, one might have supposed that the wealth of new geographical reports which flooded into Europe without a break as a result of Dutch, Portuguese, Spanish and English colonizing expeditions, from the end of the fifteenth century on, would have led very soon to the abandonment of the prevailing threefold division of the world into the Asia, Africa and Europe derived from the biblical account of the occupation of the world by Shem, Ham and Japhet, the three sons of Noah. And with them, the abandonment of Ussher's biblical timeframe.

However, that was by no means the case. For, Scholder concludes, in the history of discoveries the tenacity of old views remains one of the most astounding facts. (There is still a 'Flat Earth' Society.) The unity of Scripture, church and history offered by the old world picture would not be lightly set aside in the face of the difficulty of making sense of and imposing chronological order on new, diverse, numerous and individual accounts. The scale of change called for, in Christian imagination and self-perception, made resistance to it all the stronger. The Bible continued to be (and still continues to be for many) a presupposition for the unity of historical understanding, in that history 'as a whole' may be found in it, related to it and divided in accordance with it. All this was, and is, of course, possible only within a relatively closed sphere of western Christian cultural influence (Scholder 1990: 67–79).

This safely enshrined the idea that God's hand had, as it were, written the dramatic historical sequence contained in the Bible that began with Adam at a fixed point in time (*c*.4000 BCE), centred on Christ's birth and would end with his return at the end of time in glory and judgement. The idea about ourselves read out of this text was (and is) that with God's eye focused on, illuminating and directing us, we are the central characters in the biblical drama of salvation, playing the major role in it from beginning to end. To challenge this view was to be seen as an enemy of the human race.

Nevertheless some early challenges were mounted to the hegemony of the Christian biblical homocentric timeline. One of the earliest and most notable is a manuscript finished in 1641 but not published in book form until 1655 (five years after Ussher's calculations). Written by a French Calvinist scholar, Isaac de La Peyrère, its title, *Prae-Adamitae*, or 'Pre-Adamites', speaks for itself. It was printed first in Holland and appeared without details of printer or author, although this proved a vain precaution. During a stay in the Catholic Spanish Netherlands, he was put in prison and only released after supposedly recanting his views. The book sold like hot cakes, and was translated from the French into English and Dutch. Its success may be partly due to the extreme reactions it provoked immediately after it appeared. In 1656, after a storm of indignation, it was publicly burnt in Paris by the hangman (Scholder 1990: 82–87).

Post-Copernican challenges

What was so shocking about the book? La Peyrère's overall theory contains, among other items considered heretical, the claim that on internal evidence, such as the account of his death, Moses was not the author of the Penta-teuch. The corollary to this is that the Bible's privileged status as a text revealed by God to Moses, and therefore its relationship to the truth, was placed in question. Therefore the literal truth of the Genesis narrative, and all the doctrines built on it, was equally put in question. Second, he pro-posed that there were men and women born before Adam, and that Jewish history, not human history, began with the person called Adam. He also proposed that everyone will be saved, no matter what he or she believes or whether he or she is a pre-Adamite, an Adamite or a post-Adamite (Popkin 1977: 183).

This can certainly count among the immediate post-Copernican chal-lenges to the epistemological privilege of the Christian establishment and to the truth of its biblical interpretations. It was also the moment when reason,

or logic, or what would now be called scientific method challenged the prevailing world picture, its parameters and its preconceptions. La Peyrère's
own reading of certain biblical texts gave him, he felt, a valid alternative,
one he was bound to seek given, as I said, that he embodied the conflict
between revealed truth and what we now call scientific reasoning. He used
his own interpretation (against accepted readings) to offer biblical proof as
well as compelling arguments for, first, the existence of men before Adam
(otherwise why did God bother to mark Cain and where did Cain get his
wife?) and, second, as to 'why the establishment of the earth cannot be
derived from that beginning usually associated with Adam'.

His scientific method, as it would now be understood, was to base his
arguments for the pre-existence of human beings before Adam on ancient
Chaldean calculations; on the earliest documents from Egypt, Ethiopia and
Scythia; on the existence of newly discovered lands, including those such as
China, Mexico and Tasmania whose inhabitants 'probably' did not descend
from Adam. This use of external, that is extra-ecclesiastical, authorities
marks a turning point in the relationship between what might be called the
appeal to reason, or certainly to scientific method, and the appeal to biblical
or traditional religious authority. Augustine's dismissal of the possible existence of the Antipodes and their inhabitants could not be held true by men
who had been to Tasmania or New Zealand (Popkin 1977: 184–185;
Scholder 1990: 86–89).

The furore raised by the book may astonish us now rather more than its
content. But it indicates how revolutionary it is to use geological rather
than 'Christian' dating – or 'earth history' rather than Ussher's 'salvation
history' – as the context for our worldview. And how revolutionary it can be
even to juxtapose the two. For, after Copernicus, the epistemological privilege of neither one nor the other can be maintained absolutely. Each has its
own sphere, its own grounds on which to make assertions. And, in both
cases, its knowledge base, curtailed as it is by the bounds of our being
human, is necessarily incomplete.

Nowhere is that more evident than in the years between Copernicus and
Newton. As we saw with the anthropic principle, the difference between
scientific ground and assertion is as important for science as it is for religion.
For, while it is a fact that there is now intelligent life on earth, whatever
assertion is made on the basis of that fact (for example, that the universe
evolved in order that human intelligence might emerge) cannot claim to be
absolutely true because our knowledge is not exhaustive or absolute,
however much we might like it to be.

It is a theological axiom that, by our very nature, and the nature we
impute to God, our knowledge of God is always incomplete. Luther stated
categorically that God could neither be grasped nor measured; could not be

located yet was present in all places simultaneously (Dillenberger 1988: 35). Theologically, therefore, because it is a historical fact attested by accepted authorities such as Josephus and Trajan that a man called Jesus died under Pontius Pilate, we may assert that a man with this name lived and died at a particular moment in time. Whatever further assertion is made on the basis of that fact (for example, that he was the only Son of God) cannot claim to be *absolutely* true. Our knowledge about him is necessarily incomplete. And any claim to epistemological privilege which implicitly or explicitly denies that incompleteness rightly invites scepticism. At the very least, those who claim the privilege must answer for its use. Above all, do they use it to inflict violence in defence of the power their privilege bestows (Primavesi 2000: 140–147)?

What is at stake here is the equation of the whole 'truth' – about the universe or about the earth, about ourselves or above all about God – with any one form of human knowledge, however categorized. This unknowability is not to be confused with mere ignorance. It points towards an absolute limit to what we can say we know or what can be spoken. James Carse links it to what the mystic Meister Eckhart called 'a higher ignorance'. It is knowing that, from within the unfinished circle of our present knowledge, there is no way of knowing what keeps that knowledge forever incomplete. It is the awareness that even the simplest of our certainties are laced with mystery and surprise. '*This* ignorance, says Eckhart, does not come from lack of knowledge but rather it is from knowledge that one may achieve this ignorance' (Carse 1994: 59).

What is also being put in question is the *use* of knowledge by any group privileged by possessing it. For who would not listen to those who say they have privileged access to 'the truth' when their voice resounds with the power to act on it? The darker side of this claim to possession of 'truth' is, of course, the disempowerment of those whose claims are denied, silenced or not even considered.

In the outbreak of foot-and-mouth disease in Great Britain, the chief scientist spoke for the scientific establishment on behalf of the government. His authoritative voice advised and decided on the literally devastating slaughter policy. The alternative voices of other scientists, farmers, animal welfare groups and concerned people everywhere, calling for vaccination rather than slaughter to be used on healthy animals, went unreported in most of the mainstream media. As, at the time, did the government's change in policy on this and the grounds for it. The privileging by political authority of certain types of human knowledge reduced all others to that state of 'dumbness' which disempowered the animals themselves so effectively and so devastatingly. The scale and scope of this exercise of almost total control over millions of animals is, to go back to the Introduction, 'something new under the sun'. But its roots go back to that tenacious idea we have about ourselves and our God-given supremacy, which the original Copernican challenge scarcely touched. The question now facing us is how rooted that idea still is. And while the challenge to it again comes from within the scientific establishment, resistance to the challenge also comes most effectively from there.

However, the weapon of silencing (still employed by the Church against dissident theologians) is also effectively used by and against scientists today. As well as the media silence imposed on some of them, as in the case of foot-and-mouth disease, it is highly effective in the system known as 'peer review' where scientific papers in leading journals are accepted or rejected for publication. That acceptance or rejection has consequences for careers in science, where publications weigh heavily in job applications. James Lovelock had a long struggle to get his work on Gaia theory published. The 'dumbing' of dissent now within science is most effective, however, where academic scientific research is funded and therefore controlled by major economic interests, for example, in agribusiness, mining or pharmaceutical corporations. Which, in turn, as we saw, wield real influence over governments. Rachel Carson's experiences with Velsicol, Monsanto and the National Agricultural Chemicals Association in the United States in the early 1960s is an exemplary case (Hynes 1989: 115–139; Lear 1997: 428–448).

Theological challenges

Going back to the time immediately after Copernicus, there was no uniformly positive or negative institutional response to his views. Generally speaking, theologians simply continued to elaborate the traditional view of the world, while among mathematicians, astronomers and metaphysicians active in university circles, some rejected and others defended or used his work. Until Galileo, the responses were individual rather than along institutional lines (Dillenberger 1988: 71–74). One of the most notable was that of Thomas Digges who, in 1576, embraced the Copernican revision enthusiastically and carried it to the exciting astronomical conclusion that modern science has shown to be correct: that the universe is infinite. Giordano Bruno, however, was the one who, before his death at the stake in 1600, most forcefully and publicly argued for this move 'from a closed to an infinite universe' (Koyré 1957: 32–48). Other astronomers, the most famous being Tycho Brahe, kept the traditional Ptolemaic view of the earth as being in a central and unmoved position, but used Copernicus's mathematics to argue for the sun and moon rotating around the earth while the other planets move around the sun (Kuhn 1957: 202f.).

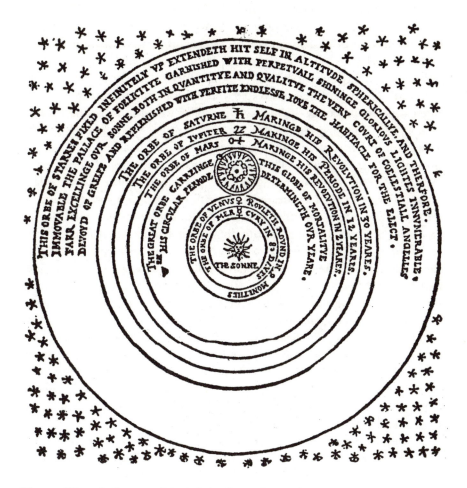

Thomas Digges's diagram of the infinite Copernican universe.

After Galileo, however, theologians and scientists were faced, it seemed, with the choice between two truths, both claiming their allegiance. As we saw, it was now that the Roman Catholic Church condemned the truth of Copernican theory. Kepler, a Protestant, could and did deal with the problem by keeping a low profile, that is, by writing, as Copernicus had done, for experts. He had to do this because institutional Protestantism no less than Roman Catholicism rejected Copernican theory. In 1596 Kepler published a draft set of mathematical proofs for the Copernican system which could only be understood by experts like his teacher Maestlin at

Tübingen, himself a Copernican. In 1598 he wrote to Maestlin: 'What shall we do? The whole of astronomy is not worth causing offence to one of Christ's little ones. . . . Let us communicate our view candidly to anyone who approaches us privately. In public let us keep silent. Why should we destroy astronomy by astronomy?' (Scholder 1990: 157n36).

Yet for Kepler truth was indivisible. Indeed, for him, this integrity constituted what he called its 'holiness'. 'But holier to me is the truth which I demonstrate from philosophy, that the earth is round and is inhabited at the antipodes, that it is quite insignificant and small and finally that it is borne through the stars – with all due respect to the doctors of the church' (Scholder 1990: 90). Interestingly, La Peyrère used almost the same language: 'For although I am dearest to myself, the truth is a greater friend to me'. The way out of this dilemma that Kepler chose was to say that scripture does not aim to communicate physical or mathematical facts but the revelation of God's greatness and glory. And at the same time to say that the truth demonstrated by mathematics will hold up against all authorities (Scholder 1990: 54, 157n36, 90). In words almost identical to Kepler's, Calvin sees theology no longer in competition with astronomy but as operating within different limits. Those limits have to be respected and that means staying within the field of one's competence. But ultimately all fields of knowledge were but different methods of illuminating their common object, the glory of God (Oberman 1986: 186f.). This was an attempt, valid in a Christian culture, not only to resolve one's own internal struggle between faith and reason, but also to avert any suggestion that they postulated a double truth.

However unsatisfactory this solution may now appear, especially when facts discerned by reason cannot be reconciled with a certain kind of faith based on a literal interpretation of biblical texts (as in evolutionary history), it has often been resorted to by scientists and theologians alike. Even though they would hold, now as then, that its primary aim is safeguarding the indivisibility of truth. That remains important, and to lose sight of its importance is to lose sight of Kepler's sound instinct that the disciplines of theology and science have different functions and different areas of expertise rather than a different goal. The goal itself may be described as 'the truth', but it is not disclosed in its wholeness to any one discipline. In his lifetime, theology held the position of privilege and assimilated all claims to truth to itself. Now, as demonstrated in the anthropic principle and the foot-and-mouth crisis in Great Britain, the balance has shifted the other way and epistemological privilege is generally accorded to science. In both cases problems arise when it is presupposed that any system of human knowledge, or even any combination of systems, can adequately and absolutely express the holiness or wholeness of truth.

For theologians, this means that whatever questions are raised, or rephrased, whether by Copernicus, Darwin or Lovelock, they cannot be safely – and the emphasis here is on security, stability and certainty in all its forms – confined within the (assumed) parameters of a biblical history said to begin with an individual 'Adam' and to culminate in Christ. And further, that the authority which claims that putative timespan as definitive for all preceding or subsequent earth history cannot be absolutized, nor can its attendant claims for our being the sole centre of significance within that history.

Galileo's challenge

It is (relatively) easy for me to say this now. But as we know, it was very different for Galileo, different even from how it was for Copernicus or Kepler. An obvious difference is that the political and physical power of the Roman Catholic Church was ineffective against the person of the Protestant Kepler. Nor could the defunct Copernicus be thrown in prison until he recanted, as was La Peyrère. Galileo differed from Kepler in another important respect. Kepler, as we saw, made a conscious decision to communicate only with experts and in expert language. Galileo, however, spoke to everyone. It was essentially the greater accessibility and ease of understanding of his proofs that made them the focus of attention and brought him into the centre of the argument.

There is an interesting parallel here with Darwin. Both he and Galileo would now be known as public intellectuals, making new and exciting theories available to the widest possible readership. Galileo's *Sidereal Messenger* reported 'for everyone' direct observations revealing great and most marvellous phenomena observed through his telescope (Scholder 1990: 54). Darwin was read as someone telling a new story and his *Origin of Species* was 'widely and thoroughly *read* by his contemporaries' (Beer 2000: 3). Similarly Lovelock and Margulis write in a very accessible style and have been widely read and translated.

However, then as now, the very ease of reading provoked attack. As Scholder says, the unity of worldview and faith associated with the power of tradition, backed up by the authority of scripture and given life by the trust and hope of many generations, could not be 'refuted' overnight even by the most compelling evidence. And it says much for the power of tradition that the earlier advocates of the new worldview all without exception sought to prove that their results did not infringe the authority of scripture. It also says much for the power of the new ideas that their defenders had the courage to put them forward in the face of real physical danger (Scholder 1990: 91).

For consensus is always stronger than dissent. So Galileo had to find support for his ideas wherever possible. In reaction to the attacks on them he defended himself to the great and the good of his day, notably in a letter in 1615 to Christina of Lorraine, widow of the Grand Duke of Tuscany and mother of his patron, Cosimo Medici II. In a reprise of Kepler's argument about the different functions of scripture and science, Galileo showed his literary skills with a witty play on words, saying that the aim of the Holy Spirit is to teach us how to go to heaven, not how the heavens 'go'. He also made a distinction between 'knowledge that can be demonstrated and knowledge which allows of opinions', that is, of interpretations. In contrast to the statements of scripture, he says, the regularities of nature do not depend on our interpretation but come about independently of us. They are removed from human whim and act in accordance with eternal, unchangeable laws. (But there again, I would want to enter the caveat that our discernment of those laws must always remain open to question.) Scripture, however, does not address such compelling truths. Its statements need interpretation and are at the mercy of human whim and ignorance.

Whatever his intentions, by denying scripture and tradition all competence in scientific questions, Galileo was at the same time claiming a new principle of knowledge outside the jurisdiction of the Church. In the context of his time, this was tantamount to claiming power hitherto vested in the Church. And the claim was made, not in the name of God, but in the name of reason. This at a time when the facts appealed to by reason (as in the case of the pre-Adamites) had become important for church and for theology. Therefore anyone who wanted to dispute this claim had to dispute the facts. That, says Scholder, was one of the reasons why Christian theology of all persuasions refused for more than a century to recognize the new facts resulting from Galileo's experiments.

So in March 1610 Copernicus's work was 'suspended' by the Vatican for further examination, and in 1616 was placed on the Index where it remained until 1822. This decision was based on the opinion that

> the statement 'The sun is the centre of the world and consequently does not move in space' was declared to be 'foolish and absurd in philosophy and formally heretical, in so far as this explicitly contradicts the statements of Holy Scripture in many places according to their real wording and according to the general interpretation and understanding of the holy Fathers and learned theologians.'
>
> (Scholder 1990: 58–63)

As noted already, Copernicus did, understandably, get some things wrong. But I want to emphasize here that the express condemnation of his whole thesis seventy-three years after his death roughly coincides with the beginning of deliberate anti-Copernican polemic from the Christian churches throughout Europe. And while the explicit aim of that polemic was to safeguard the biblical frame of reference and purpose in regard to the earth and to man, the implicit aim was to block any doubt about the centrality of human beings in the universe and, by extension, about their ability to know God's will for the world. And, as we have seen, that will was interpreted as our being given control over the lives of all other species. Or more precisely, that some of us are.

All of this recalls points already made in regard to epistemological privilege, its bases, and its use of power to hold on to and strengthen those bases. I want to say here that, for me as a theologian, what matters is the way in which theological appeals to ultimate authority are implemented. Are they used to excuse or promote violence in God's name? Or, in the case of epistemologically privileged science – where resistance to the challenge to our status implicit in scientific Copernican principles is strong today – is violence excused in the name of 'the best science' (whatever that may be)? A parallel to the epistemological privileging of Ptolemaic cosmology looms afresh in the contemporary emergence of the anthropic principle. As Livio warns, its anti-Copernicanism should bother us. It is anti-Copernican in that it supports the presupposition that the purpose of earth's evolution is the working out of human destiny. It is anti-Copernican and indeed openly Platonic in that the earth is presumed to be no more than a staging post for human rationality, or for 'intelligent information processing' on our way to another kind of 'Enlightenment'.

In both cases the assumption is that all that has evolved, has evolved for us. Or in pre-Copernican terms, everything still revolves around us. And while heaven is no longer (publicly) invoked as the goal of human life, we now assume that the evolution of the universe has given us the means (through our intelligence) to create our 'heaven' here on earth and therefore the right to manipulate all other forms of life in order to enhance or prolong our own.

While it is clearly on the scientific grounds raised by Gaia theory that I, a theologian, have been impelled to challenge scientific assumptions about our position as earthlings, it is the quasi-theological presuppositions of those assumptions that are my main concern. In the following chapter I shall look at how assumptions about the nature of human knowledge affect our self-perception as well as our efforts to understand the world scientifically – and theologically.

4   The incomplete revolution

Previous chapters brought us from a Ptolemaic, geocentric view of the universe to a Newtonian, heliocentric one, and on from there to that imaged for us today by the latest in space technology. This present view of the universe is explored by experts in astrophysics who assure us that, in fact, it has no centre. Our starting point, sixteenth-century Cracow, saw Copernicus poring over mathematical tables in order to reach his revolutionary conclusions. Now we listen to scientists who reach theirs by using computer data relayed back to earth from the edges of our solar system and beyond by the Hubble Space Telescope.

Reflecting on this historic journey and the people encountered on the way, one thing strikes me forcibly. Whichever guide was consulted, at whatever moment in time, all of them were ready and willing, even eager, to guide us to a place where they themselves had never been. All were anxious to tell us about our solar system, or our galaxy, not from a new or further vantage point they themselves had reached within it, but from one they, and we, had never left. We all share a common starting point that for them, as for us, is also our common finishing point: earth. Whatever directions we are given for reaching beyond our solar system, or whatever descriptions are given of what we might see on arrival there, all are given to and offered us by those who do all their travelling without leaving location earth. And that is likely to remain the case for the foreseeable future.

This means that we routinely set out to follow a *Hitch-hiker's Guide to the Galaxy* written and handed to us by a hitch-hiker who never left home. When we look at Ptolemaic or Copernican diagrams, or at the latest images from Hubble, we generally disregard the fact that they all originate on earth, the former produced through the power of thought and imagination and the latter similarly, although enhanced by technology. The views of Mars beamed back to us by the latest Mars Explorer come from certain data programmed here in one way rather than another that is then interpreted by those who receive it back here on earth. Neither Hubble, Carter, Tipler nor

Livio, any more than Ptolemy, Copernicus, Galileo, Kepler or Newton, have ever viewed the universe or its systems from any other location. None of them claim to have had an out-of-body experience that would enable them to do so. Therefore the universe they depict for us is one none of them have visited or seen for themselves. They, and we through their eyes, see a universe that we cannot see from earth.

'So what?' you might ask. Isn't their view supported by more and more information gleaned from space exploration? But for reasons that will emerge more clearly throughout this chapter I want to draw attention to the fact that, in order for Ptolemy or Copernicus to imagine what the universe (or the earth) really looks like, in common with them any of us who wish to do the same must apparently disregard the limitations imposed on us by our own bodily make-up and by our location. We must apparently ignore or at least try to compensate for the fact that we see it only through bodily eyes and from an earth-centred body: from the point of view of a 'self' centred on earth.

Kant deals with this cognitive dilemma by proposing a Copernican revolution in philosophy: that 'we do what Copernicus did ... when he found he could make no progress by assuming that all the heavenly bodies revolved around the spectator. He reversed the process and tried the experiment of assuming that the spectator revolved while the stars remained at rest' (Kant 1924: xxix). In other words, we deal with the fact that our knowledge is self-centred by accepting that our location and our personal faculties of sight, hearing, reason and the ability to derive abstract concepts from concrete experience play an indispensable role in any understanding we have of that experience – and that all of this necessarily colours and shapes any representation we make of it.

So when scientists now declare that the universe has no centre, they necessarily ignore the fact that they themselves have not journeyed through it and found no centre there. And that they make their declaration from a heliocentric viewing point that is itself centred on earth. Nevertheless they make their declaration about the nature of the universe confident of their competence to assess the evidence available to them. Their confidence in human knowledge (and in their possession of it in one of its most refined forms) is very evident in the development of the anthropic principle. Its necessary presupposition is that we are able to know why, as well as how, the universe has evolved. Its immediate presupposition is that human observations, understanding and representations of its present state are sufficient for scientists to know its origins and purpose. This means that they are as ready now to argue scientifically as the Vatican is theologically for our being truly the centre of importance in the universe because we are the purpose of its evolution.

Bearing all this in mind I want first to look more closely at the nature of human observation; at its necessary role in scientific knowledge as disclosure of facts about the world and how this affects conclusions drawn from it and truth claims for it. Then I shall go on to examine Copernicus's own observations and the way in which his particular frame of reference, which combined scientific and religious preconceptions, led to his heliocentric view of the universe. Finally I want to make a distinction between human knowledge of the world (whether scientific or religious) and omniscience; this last in the sense of total knowledge about the world or indeed about anything else. At various stages I shall link this claim to omniscience to Freud's claim that science, in the persons of Copernicus and Darwin, dealt a definitive blow to an original hope for our own transcendent importance in the universe.

Observing the universe

In order to see the universe as 'correctly' as possible, we must, as we have seen, apparently disregard – or in the astronauts' case, displace – what centres us within it: our bodies. We must put to one side those bodily sense impressions which bind us irrevocably to earth. For even as our eyes tell us (in the northern hemisphere) that the sun, the moon and the stars rise daily in the east and travel across the sky to set in the west (both points named in this way relative to our location on earth) we are re-minded by our intellects (and by our experience of overnight flying) that this commonplace view, commonly assented to and employed, is mistaken. Simultaneously, we believe and disbelieve what we see before us. Simultaneously, we identify with and differentiate between what we know with our bodily senses and what is the actual state of affairs. And just to add to the confusion, in the latter case, how 'hard' science routinely describes the universe (that is, how scientists see it) in terms of what their eyes tell them and us about their earthly environment.

I have long been fascinated by the coloured images of the universe coming back to us from the Hubble Telescope. When I asked whether or not the colours are truly representative of what is in space, I was told by my scientist husband that, at best, they correspond to the wavelengths reflected back to us from there but are quite likely to have been 'computer enhanced'. But who decides that 'red' light has a frequency of about 460 trillion waves per second or how wavelengths should be 'enhanced'? Who sees and names the colours as red, yellow and purple? (See Sagan 1997: 47–54; Schroedinger 2000: 123–127, 158–164.) I remember being told (by someone who had lived there) that some tribes in Nigeria have no concept of the colour 'red' and therefore what we call 'red' is missing from their cloth dyes and art. How would *they* name 460 trillion light waves per second or depict the Hubble data?

This draws attention to the subjective nature of our representations of what we 'see': whether in the sky immediately above us or, through a telescope, what is beyond the range of our eyesight. It is always represented from the perspective of a particular human individual or group. Depending on the actual point of view of any individual, a square may appear as a square, or as a diamond or, if viewed from a central position below or within it, as a triangle. Uranus and its rings may appear, as they do on my 2002 calendar of Hubble images, like a sphere within an ellipse of light reflected from the sun. In fact the accompanying notes tell me that, although they appear bright in the image, the rings reflect only about 4 per cent of the sunlight that falls on them, making them as dark as soot or coal (Universe of the Hubble Space Telescope 2002 Calendar, published by astroGraphics Publishing, www.astrographics.com).

Whatever scene I confront I can adopt different vantage points from which it will assume different shapes – the hologram effect. So whatever picture or representation I use to describe it is variable: conceptualized or ordered *by me* (and therefore potentially by others too) in a particular way at a particular time according to certain personal criteria. I am the source of the representation and present it as seen from my 'perspective'. Through this lens or grid I impose an order on what is before me that allows me to represent not the scene itself, but my perspective on it.

There is yet another factor to be considered in scientific representations based on observations. Choices are made not only about how the observed phenomena will be described, and by whom, but also about which phenomena are chosen for observation and representation. Those choices depend on the observer's particular frame of reference. And that, we shall see, may and often does include phenomena that are not actually observed. Nevertheless these may and often do play an important part in what is eventually represented.

Copernicus's observations and frame of reference

Astronomer Owen Gingerich begins his commentary on Noel Swerdlow's analysis of Copernicus's own observations with a remark about the mystique attached to 'observations'. They are, he says, supposedly the direct path to truth. He illustrates how treacherous this path is by recounting a conversation between Einstein and Heisenberg recorded in the latter's autobiography:

> 'But you don't seriously believe', Einstein protested, 'that none but observable magnitudes must go into a physical theory?'
>
> 'Isn't that precisely what you have done with relativity?' Heisenberg asked in some surprise.

'Possibly I did use this kind of reasoning,' Einstein admitted, 'but it is nonsense all the same. . . . [O]n principle, it is quite wrong to try founding a theory on observable magnitudes alone. In reality the very opposite happens. It is the theory which decides what we can observe. You must appreciate that observation is a very complicated process.'

(Gingerich 1975: 99)

Gingerich recounts this episode before commenting on the fact that Copernicus had only a few ancient Ptolemaic observations available to him to which he added a minimum number of his own. Among them were three 'observed' planetary oppositions that he presented as differing from those of Ptolemy, two of them falling in the daytime 'when the planet [Mercury] is below the horizon!' This reminds us, says Gingerich, that to decide precisely when and where the opposition occurs one must know the position of the sun as well as the position of the planet.

In fact, for Copernicus as well as Ptolemy, it was necessary to reckon the position of the fictitious mean sun and not the true sun; this is related to the circumstance that Copernicus used the centre of the earth's orbit, rather than the physical sun, as the centre for his system. Hence, all these observations are at least one step removed from the actual sighting of the planet in the sky.

(Gingerich 1975: 99–101)

This explains my earlier remark (p. 17) about mistakes made by Copernicus that meant at least parts of his heliocentric theory could be dismissed on the grounds of inaccuracy. Swerdlow and Gingerich supply mathematical evidence of this. The point I want to stress about Copernicus's observations is that they were understood by him within the framework of his solar theory. And further, that the theory itself did not depend on the *true* position of the sun relative to all the other planets but relative only to the earth's orbit. The representations of those observations were made within a frame of reference that did not actually include or support all of them. Yet his *understanding* of what he observed, based on his solar theory, worked sufficiently well for him to discriminate between it and that offered by Ptolemy. And for his to count eventually as more accurate – in spite of its 'appalling inaccuracies' (Gingerich 1975: 104f.).

Brief as it is, this account of Copernican method shows how scientific observations, then and now, are actually recorded and then amplified, accepted or rejected. They are never recorded, amplified, accepted or rejected from the point of view of no-one in particular. Both Ptolemy and Copernicus had a scientific frame of reference that allowed them to concentrate their attention and that of others on what they deemed to be the most important aspect of what they observed. Even to the point, in both cases, of claiming to have observed things they could not possibly have observed. This was not done in order to deceive but to advance the claims of a theory about the universe that they believed to be true to the facts. The entire exercise was carried out by Copernicus, says Gingerich, primarily to show 'that the heliocentric cosmology was compatible with reasonable planetary predictions rather than to reform the inaccuracies of astronomical predictions'. This conclusion is given added weight by recently discovered evidence that shows Copernicus was not himself unaware of major discrepancies between prediction and observation (Gingerich 1975: 104f.).[4]

This brief excursion into the nature of Copernicus's particular perception of the universe allows me to make an essential point about his heliocentrism. Because he took the fixed stars – stars that retain the same relative position with respect to one another – as his fixed frame of reference for planetary motion, he perceived that the earth is moving around the sun rather than the other way round. And because he took the centre of the earth's orbit rather than the physical sun as the centre of his system, he made the sun, as viewed from earth, central to the universe.

Because he changed his frame of reference from that of Ptolemy, he changed his perception of the sun's position. However, at the risk of stating the obvious, the sun's actual position in the universe did not change. Nor did everyone's experience of earth's immobility. Nevertheless, everyone's perception of the sun's position changed over a relatively short length of time. As it did, the common frame of reference for ourselves within the universe became and has remained heliocentric – even though we know now that, in strict astronomical terms, the sun is not 'the centre' of our planetary system. And even though, then and now, the change goes against the evidence of our senses. What did not change at all after Copernicus (*pace* Freud) was the common perception of our own central importance. If anything, for reasons I shall come to, heliocentrism enlarged rather than shrank that perception.

Darwin too changed the frame of reference for looking at our species' position by placing our evolution within that of all life on earth. That changed his perception of our position. The position itself did not change: we have always been and still are earth-centred mammals with a common ancestry stretching back some eight million years out of four billion years or so of life on earth. We share 99.4 per cent of our DNA with chimpanzees. These physical facts did not change with or after Darwin. What did begin to change (for many of us) was the frame of reference for our perception of our species' position – and so it is now (mostly) acceptable to describe ourselves as I have done here. But to date what has scarcely changed (*pace* Freud again) is the commonplace perception of the unique importance of our species both on earth and in the universe.

Lovelock's frame of reference in Gaia theory is the role of the earth's environment in the emergence and evolution of life and, after that emergence, the role played by life, in interaction with the global environment, in creating and maintaining earth's environment. That is (very slowly) becoming the frame of reference within which we are now being forced (by environmental change) and enabled (through environmental and social sciences) to perceive ourselves. Neither the role of living beings nor of the environment has changed. However, our perception of both roles – and in particular of their interconnectedness – is gradually changing as we experience, observe and deepen our understanding of their interactive effects.[5]

What did not change then, after Copernicus, what has not yet changed to any great degree after Darwin and what needs to change after Lovelock is the commonplace perception of our species' exceptional status. In my terms, the Copernican change from a geocentric to a heliocentric universe has not been accompanied by a shift away from homocentrism. To understand why this is the case it helps to go back to Copernicus himself and ask why his astronomical perspective changed. Then we may judge how that change affected his – and our – perception of human importance.

Copernicus's overall frame of reference

In his preface to the *De Revolutionibus*, Copernicus says quite clearly that he is reacting to what he saw as wrong in Ptolemy's perspective and, consequently, in his representation of the heavens. Copernicus's 'principal consideration' is 'the structure of the universe and *the true symmetry* of its parts' (my italics). For him and for Renaissance writers in general the symmetry in question is related first and foremost to the whole human body: to the 'symmetrical harmony' between forearm and foot, palm and finger. Instead of this, Copernicus says, Ptolemy depicts hands, feet, a head and other pieces: fragments that do not belong to one another at all; so that 'a monster rather than a man would be put together from them' (Copernicus 1992: 4). (This sensitivity to bodily symmetry may have been heightened by Copernicus's study of medicine.)

His language about the Ptolemaic cosmic 'body' reveals that his was as much an aesthetic and religious reaction as a scientific one. Indeed, as we have seen, from the point of view of its agreement with the empirical data or its predictive utility, the Copernican system presented no real advantage over its geocentric rivals. 'Its superiority resides chiefly in the coherence it introduced into planetary motion. No doubt this coherence is eminently significant from the point of view of scientific logic, but the fact remains that Copernicus himself presented it in an aesthetic light' (Hallyn 1997: 101).

Its 'scientific' coherence too is doubtful, I would have thought, in the light of those weaknesses in method and conclusion exposed by Gingerich and others. But that serves to strengthen rather than weaken Hallyn's point that Copernicus's reaction was an aesthetic one. He (Hallyn) gives readers the opportunity to share the Copernican aesthetic experience by juxtaposing pertinent illustrations: one of a fussily embellished Ptolemaic astronomical map in which the signs of the Zodiac and the planetary orbits jostle for attention; the latter requiring further mapping with epicycles in order to explain how their differing distances from earth affect their trajectories.

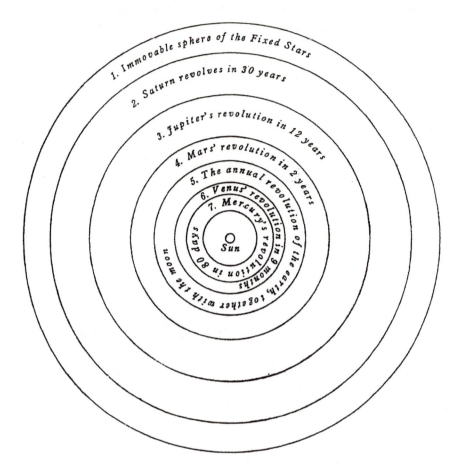

In sharp contrast is the serenely radical and aesthetically coherent simplicity of the Copernican heliocentric diagram.

Hallyn also juxtaposes a seventeenth-century illustration by Villard de Honnecourt of mechanist geometrism (illustrated as human heads without bodies as well as whole bodies of birds and animals) with a sixteenth-century Albrecht Dürer drawing of the human body. Dürer's own account of this body's symmetry states that it requires the entire image, from head to foot, to be in proportion, with the parts proportioned among each other and not 'badly thrown together'. Hallyn remarks that de Honnecourt's mechanist mathematicization is to Dürer's organicist one as Ptolemy's system is to Copernicus's. He also quotes Piero della Francesca: 'as the word implies, perspective refers to things seen from afar, represented proportionately within specific conditions *according to their distances*'. Copernicus's perspective 'combined the concept of a "symmetrical" Creation with the requirements of an organicist representation based on mathematical reason' (Hallyn 1997: 73–102. Original italics).

The point I must stress here is that, for Copernicus, the aesthetic concept of a symmetrical, organicist universe was ultimately based on his religious belief that this was how God had created it. The entire heavens were a visible symbol of divinity: in other words, their symmetry was divine and the mathematical reason creating the symmetry was divine reason. Therefore to see this symmetry properly, one needed, in some degree, to partake of divine reason. In so far as one did, since the whole universe could not properly be seen from earth, one's perspective on that whole was necessarily not earth-centred, but heaven-centred – in the double sense of 'located above and beyond earth' and 'divine'.

There are several assumptions behind Copernicus's logic here that hark back to earlier themes. The displacement of earth from the centre of the universe was, for him, both possible and necessary because it entailed displacing a monstrous, asymmetric, geocentric view of the universe and replacing it with a properly proportioned, symmetric, heliocentric and (implicitly) divine view. This was the religious basis for what Polanyi calls Copernicus's 'intellectual passion' and for his assumption that man is able to share that divine view, however partially, by using 'mathematical reason'.

Yet in Book One, Chapter 10 of *De Revolutionibus*, beneath the diagram in which he lays out the symmetrical order of the universe, Copernicus does not begin to describe it in the language of mathematical equations. Instead he praises the sun's centrality in the most lyrical terms. The sun, he says, is not inappropriately called by some people the lantern of the universe, by others its mind and by still others, its ruler. The Thrice Greatest (Hermes Trismegistus), he says, labels it a visible god, and Sophocles' Electra, the all-seeing (Copernicus 1992: 22). Citing these authorities for shifting the centre of the universe to the sun, Copernicus was keying into a larger movement that, from the fifteenth century on, and especially in Italy, gave rise to veritable sun worship based on the philosophical and religious connections made between Egypto-Hermetic sun-teachings and those of Plato, for whom the sun was the intelligible splendour or chief image of Ideas.

So Meister Eckhart, who had read none of Plato's dialogues either in the original or in translation, but was familiar with extracts from his writings in Macrobius and Neoplatonic reminiscences in Augustine, tells us that:

> when he [Plato] made bold to speak to the highest Lord of things, maintained that it is just as impossible to declare anything about God as it is difficult to find Him. Hence he took refuge in images and parables of things, and *among all created things he found nothing more similar to God than the sun, for which reason he also called Him 'the sun'.*
>
> (Clark 1957: 29–30. Italics added)

I shall come back to the Christian religious doctrines systematized in the celestial hierarchies of Pseudo-Dionysius. Here I want to stay with Frances Yates's comments on the religious and mystical importance of the sun within the contemporary worldview of Copernicus. He was not, she says, living within the thirteenth-century worldview of Thomas Aquinas but within that of the 'Platonic theologians' of Marsilio Ficino (author of the *Theologica platonica*) and their enthusiasm for the Hermetic writings. Either, she says, the intense emphasis on the sun in this new worldview was the emotional driving force that induced Copernicus to undertake his mathematical calculations, or he wished to make his discovery acceptable by presenting it within the framework of this new attitude. Perhaps, she says, both explanations, or some of each, are true. She is careful to point out, however, that Copernicus reached his epoch-making hypothesis of the revolution of the earth around the sun through pure mathematical calculation and not through the religious and magical meanings related to Ficinian sun magic read into the Copernican diagram by Giordano Bruno (Yates 1991: 153–155).

Whatever explanation we adopt for Copernicus's passionate, aesthetic and intellectual reaction to the sun's centrality there is no doubt that he drew support from and at the same time reworked an existing tradition that had developed within another cosmological framework: that of a solar myth in which Apollo, as sun god, was directly associated with the form and regular movement of the heavenly bodies. The 'Apollonian eye' still signifies a viewpoint above the earth, a view at once empowering and visionary. (Hence the naming of the Apollo Space Project.) For Copernicus it is a perspective from which divine authority and power can plausibly be seen as radiating symbolically across the earth's surface from a sacred centre (Cosgrove 2001: x, xi, 27, 57–58).

Human knowledge and total knowledge (omniscience)

As I have shown above, implicit in Copernicus's representation of the universe is the claim that, alone in the universe, man's (mathematical) reason is capable of understanding or sharing in divine reason. This ultimate religious claim to epistemological privilege went (and still goes) against the epistemological humility required by the opposite religious conviction: that it is impossible for us to discover the purposes behind the impenetrable workings (symmetrical or otherwise) of God's absolute power in the world. After all, why should God be bound by the constraints of human understanding, whether couched in mathematics or in notions of symmetry? Does the word 'God' not imply One bound by no human constraint? From this more modest religious perspective, all we can do is to accumulate astronomical or other types of knowledge about the ways in which God's absolute power is displayed in the universe. This may take us to the threshold, as it were, of that divine power but not beyond into its mysterious purposes.

The important distinction between God's impenetrable, absolute power and the inscrutable ways in which it is displayed in the world was understood by Thomas Aquinas, Meister Eckhart and other religious scholars as that between the study of things that are above us (*quae supra nos*) and 'the necessarily vain desire to know the intentions of God, the One who is above us' (*qui supra nos*). (This attitude, as we saw in the discussion of the anthropic principle, characterized the worldview of Luther, Galileo and Descartes.) The distinction assumes that our desire to have full knowledge of God's intentions is both part of being human and at the same time necessarily vain. It is vain because it is impossible for human nature to penetrate fully or to understand comprehensively the workings of God's absolute power (*potentia absoluta*). This power makes everything in the universe possible that does not (according to human logic) entail self-contradiction in God. Its absolute nature means that our understanding of this power at work in the origins of heaven and earth always necessarily remains incomplete.

Nevertheless, theologians as well as scientists may and do assume that, even if we cannot hope to elaborate a satisfactory deductive and necessary cosmology, we can see, understand and accumulate descriptive knowledge of the way in which God displays divine power in the actual order of things (*potentia ordinata*), such as the determinate laws of motion (Westman 1975: 181n36, 182; Hallyn 1997: 41–43).

But there is an important proviso attached to this assumption. Science in fact advances by presuming that we can and do make mistakes in our understanding of the natural order. Imre Lakatos and Elie Zohar make this point in an essay whose title, *Why Did Copernicus' Research Program Supersede Ptolemy's?* speaks for itself. They posit 'continuous appraisal' as an essential component in scientific method and so assume that as one hypothesis or theory is (eventually) seen to be inadequate, if not mistaken, it is superseded by another (Lakatos 1975: 354–383).[6]

Theology generally assumes (notionally at least) that there is an epistemological gap between what we can say we know about God and/or about God's purposes and God's own knowledge of these or, indeed, of anything else. This distinction between the scope of human knowledge and divine omniscience is a working assumption for me. It means accepting the 'unspeakability' of those purposes that must be kept in mind when, as we do, we say what we can about them. Therefore when we do speak about them, we must use metaphor and paradox to bridge the gap between those purposes and what we can say about them (Primavesi 2000: 29–32). The frailty of these forms of language, given our tendency to take them literally, only allows us to advance cautiously towards the unnameable if not totally unknown. For the proper human aspiration to total knowledge, driven by and evidenced in our constant passion to know more, is tempered, as Meister Eckhart warned (and it is worth repeating the warning) by knowing that from within the unfinished circle of our present knowledge there is no way of knowing what keeps that knowledge forever incomplete (Carse 1994: 59f.).

This reminded me of the uncompromising statement of this truth in the opening verses of the *Tao Te Ching*:

> Tao that can be spoken of
> Is not the Everlasting Tao.
> Name that can be named,
> Is not the Everlasting name.
> Nameless, the origin of heaven and earth;
> Named, the mother of ten thousand things.

In Ellen Chen's translation of and commentary on this classic Chinese text she highlights its central message: the limitations of language – whether theological or scientific – in conveying the nature of ultimate reality. She quotes Bergson's view that 'language is invented to express and deal with the determinate and immobile'. So the everlasting, transcending all determination, cannot be spoken of or named. While all religions speak of the Absolute as beyond speech and name, the *Tao Te Ching*, she says, is unique in the reason it gives for this. The everlasting transcends the infinite not because it is 'a being than which no greater can be conceived' (Anselm), but because it is a cyclical movement or becoming.

This difference is not as important here as her conclusion that there are two postures a person may take in relation to Tao (or God) and the world. One may either view the world in its hidden aspect in Tao, or view Tao in its visible aspect as the world. This for me is an oblique parallel to Luther's distinction between the visible and invisible things of God, one he used to attack the pretentiousness of scholastic theologians who claimed to be able to describe God's attributes. Luther bases the distinction between the visible and invisible things of God on an episode in Moses's life. Moses asks to see God's glory and is told to stand in the cleft of a rock where he will be covered with God's hand while God's glory passes by. Then the hand will be taken away and Moses will see God's back. For no one can see God's face and live (Chen 1989: 51f.; Exodus 33:18–23).

Copernicus, however, was not living within Luther's worldview – or that of the *Tao Te Ching* – but within the scholastic Neoplatonic and Hermetic worldview of Marsilio Ficino, who, in his *Theologica platonica*, celebrated man's ability to reconstitute and represent the world. This proud optimism is evident in Copernicus's attempt, as an astronomer, to reconstruct astronomy in a manner that would reconcile it with cosmology and signify man's dignity and responsibility as 'beneficiary of a world created for us' (Copernicus 1992: 4; Hallyn 1997: 56).

Heliocentrism and homocentrism

Those last two words, '*for us*', signal an important religious component in Copernicus's frame of reference. The assumption behind them attempts to close the epistemological gap between the things we know about God and what God knows about all things: between what we observe in the universe and the purposes behind it. By claiming that God has made the universe, as perceived *by* us, *for* us, Copernicus assumes that he knows why God made the world. And behind that lies another claim: that the heliocentric perspective is the right one for us to adopt because it accords or is symmetrical with human reason. To declare that the world, the divine handiwork of God, was created *for us* and for our use implies that it is made so that we can understand it, represent it properly and use it for our purposes. Copernicus uses the formula (*propter nos*) in his dedicatory Preface to the Pope in order to present astronomy's failure up to his time as something by no means God-given and unavoidable, 'but rather as a scandal that is to be vividly felt as such'. Therefore: 'his appeal to the world-formula is not so much in support of his particular thesis of the Earth's motion as it is in support of the unrestricted claim he makes for astronomical cognition' (Blumenberg 1987: 172–174, 179–208).

But unrestricted perspective can rightly only be claimed by God. Therefore, implicitly at least, for Copernicus human reason is not 'geocentred': not centred on or bound by the limitations of earthly matter. (The Platonic overtones of this are evident.) As a Roman Catholic cleric he believed the Church's claim that man alone is made in the image of divine reason. His image of the universe as a symmetrical *body* is literally imaged on man's body: a macrocosm imaged on the human (male) microcosm. But for Copernicus – with resonances of the doctrine of original sin – it is the image of a macrocosmic body whose integrity must be restored. By man.

This great effort on his part was motivated, as I said already, by an understanding of God: of God as 'the supreme artificer, craftsman or artisan creator', whose divine handiwork in the creation of man displayed a symmetry that reflected the divine nature (Copernicus 1992: 18, 22). And by the belief that that symmetry is reflected in and can be appreciated, in some measure, by human nature. All of which argues for some measure of shared symmetry between the universe, God and man: between a universe and a God made in man's image.

The powerful and explicit use by Copernicus of what was then a traditional Christian belief not only resonates with the implicit religious claim to man being the centre of the universe. It also resonates with the traditional religious belief expressed in the credal statement that, '*for us men* and for our salvation' Christ came down from heaven. This highlights another element in the heliocentric perspective. It is vertically authenticated by our looking 'up': to the sun and to God in heaven. Like the sun, 'God's eye' looks down on us (and implicitly on us alone). So although man's place (earth) is no longer the geometrical centre of the universe, his profound 'centrality' along this vertical axis – and so within the sphere of the universe – remains. For heliocentrism supposedly makes it possible to distinguish several centres or midpoints along a vertical axis that divide the universe into qualitatively different regions, with that of most value at the top.

So while quantitatively the geometric centre of the sphere of the universe corresponds to the earth's centre, the lowest, heaviest, least dignified place, there are two other centres or midpoints to be found along the axis that links the earth's centre to the circumference of the Copernican universe. The earth's surface, situated halfway between the centre of the universe and the centre of the moon, is the middle of the 'physical' universe. The sun, however, occupies the middle of the 'metaphysical' universe around which the planets are ranged as around a king. Of these three centres, the sun is incontestably pre-eminent, because it is the highest. In Christian art Christ/Apollo appears in the sphere of the sun, but also and most prominently *above* the highest circle (Hallyn 1997: 131–132). Not only Christ, but everyone else, must come 'down' to earth.

Here again the traditional hierarchies allied to the Christocentrism of western culture played an important part in sanctioning and reinforcing homocentrism even as astronomical geocentrism declined. The qualitative vertical axis described above was and is the backbone of all hierarchical/monarchical systems in western culture, with God/Christ/monarch supreme at the top. Louis XIV was happy to be known as 'the Sun-King'. In the religious celestial hierarchies systematized by Pseudo-Dionysius, the Christian Trinity reigned supreme at the topmost point of the axis. Immediately below it came the ranked choirs of angels. Below them in descending order of importance and value came man, then woman, then other species, and at the bottom, earth, with those nearest to earth of least value (Primavesi 1991: 92–106, 144–146. For a discussion of Pseudo-Dionysius's celestial hierarchies and their effects, see also Primavesi 2001: 121–144).

In Renaissance art and cartography, and in religious art generally, the space beyond the sun, beyond the region of fire, the Empyrean, is encompassed by or assigned to God the Father. Christ's body, raised from earth into and beyond the heavens at his 'ascension' after death is taken as the point of intersection between divinity and humanity, between celestial and earthly space and time. The resurrection/ascension of the heavenly Sun each day becomes a potent symbol of the divine Son linking heaven and earth (Cosgrove 2001: 57–58). Or, to be more precise, linking heaven and man. For while it was *propter nos homines*, for man's sake, that Christ 'came down' to earth, he did not remain there. And his resurrection/ascension into heaven embodies what was the ultimate religious hope: our own resurrection/ascension in which our geocentrism is finally and (implicitly at least) completely abandoned. While Luther and Calvin, as we saw, taught that the earth would be recreated after the final judgement by God, so that we could, if we so wished, 'come down' there for a visit, Calvin expressly declared that he didn't see why we would want to.

The architectonic force of this hierarchical tradition is visibly reinforced by church architecture (by the dome of light over the altar, itself placed at the apex of the building, and in wall and floor mosaic representations of the sun); in ritual (in the use of sun motifs on vestments and sun-shaped gold monstrances used to bless the congregation) and of course in art, both sacred and secular. Its earth-embracing symbolic force was and is transposed into Christian claims to be the global religion. Denis Cosgrove connects the consistent conflation of Christ and Apollo to 'Christianity's claim to encompass the world: like the Apollo of Virgil's fourth *Eclogue*, the risen Christ declares a redemption beyond that of a single chosen people to one of a global "fallen nature"'. Therefore unlike Aristotelian or Ciceronian concepts of human unity, or the idea of Roman citizenship extended to all free inhabitants of the Empire, 'the Christian view of humanity is potentially uncoupled from essential ties to a place-bound *community*'. Cosgrove uses Andrea Pozzo's fresco on the ceiling of St Ignatius, Rome, painted in 1694, to illustrate how the claim to 'global redemption' was the driving force behind the Jesuit missionary enterprise. Pozzo put Christ/Apollo in a central position which 'suggests an iconographic heliocentrism' through which 'the [human] soul rises in light and music from gross material ignorance toward the beatific vision [of God] via the mystical body of Christ' (Cosgrove 2001: 57, 160–161).

Homocentrism today

In these and in other ways that are not perhaps so easily discerned, the qualitative nature of the traditional hierarchies implicit within heliocentrism has been internalized in western culture. Some of these, such as the influence of the concept of heaven, will be considered in later chapters. The point I want to make here is that the Copernican change to heliocentrism reinforced rather than changed the homocentrism of Ptolemy's geocentric model of the universe. That human-centredness still manifests itself, as it did then, in downplaying the intrinsic value of the material, the physical and the terrestrial by reducing them now to what we call 'commodity value' alone. It shows in the emphasis on the necessary mobility of global human-ity in the service of 'the market' as against a sense of belonging to any particular location or life community. It fosters and relies on a system that values the human self above all others; mind above matter, reason above emotion and increasingly, and ironically, science above religion.

Religion in Copernican times conceived of the human soul as capable of rising imaginatively and spiritually above the earth: as the intersecting point between the divine and the human. Science now conceives of the human intellect as capable of understanding and using everything in the universe for our own ends. Future expeditions to Mars and to the moon are planned and sanctioned on the grounds of obtaining their mineral and chemical resources. Culturally and socially the sense of human importance supported by and along a qualitative vertical axis has led to and remains a way of valuing men above women (I have kept strictly to the androcentric language of various authors quoted); the learned and intelligent above the 'ignorant'; some 'symmetrical' bodies above those not so perceived; some 'advanced' cultures above others; and astrophysics above agriculture. And always, everywhere and in all respects, placing human concerns above those of all other forms of life on earth.

Every claim within western culture to the unique importance of human life is implicitly attached to this vertical valuation system. Though dressed in different metaphors at different times, as long as this view of ourselves per-sists it shows that the Copernican revolution to heliocentrism hasn't changed our view of ourselves. In fact, rather than outraging our naïve self-love, if anything he bolstered support for it. We moved from astronomical geocentrism via religious heliocentrism to an even more entrenched and scientifically sanctioned homocentrism.

After Darwin, too, reactions to an apparent loss of biological importance did not increase our sense of being earth-centred. The opposition to Darwin was seen for the most part as a religious reaction. Therefore the scientific homocentrism against which every other species was and is meas-ured, and their relative unimportance established, went relatively unchal-lenged and has remained so.

Now, however, after Lovelock, given our numbers and the destructive power and range of our technologies, our frame of reference for looking at our role and position within the whole earth community is gradually changing. It allows, indeed necessitates, a change in our *perception* of ourselves as uniquely privileged within the universe and, on that basis, making claims to have and to pursue a dominant role on earth. Like the original Copernican revolution, this change in our frame of reference may, in time, activate a decisive shift in our perspective on earth: one that would take our actual position on earth, (that of earth-centredness) seriously. That has not changed. To be happy with it would be a welcome and necessary change in self-perception for us.

To help it along I would like to see religious writers argue strongly for an explicit distinction between the human capacity for knowledge and omni-science as here defined: as total knowledge of the universe and its purposes. It would also help if they openly align themselves with those scientists who argue consistently for this distinction on other grounds. Otherwise our sense of human importance is further inflated with every breakthrough in science and technology, just as it was and is with religious claims about the world being made 'for us'.

For Christians the goal of all knowledge is, we are told, the God known in a mirror, darkly: the One that, in Meister Eckhart's words, sees the highest angel and a midge as of equal value (Clark 1957: 31). But what kind of God is this? The kind of God who, many different biblical writers assure us, has no favourites (Deuteronomy 10:17; Acts 34:16; Romans 2:11; James 2:1). Such impartiality, when accompanied by recognition of every being's self-worth and concern for its well-being, is necessarily attributable only to God. As one translation of the Tao puts it:

Impartiality is the highest nobility;
The highest nobility is divine;
And the divine is the Way (Tao).
(Cleary 1993: 18)

5   Revolution within ourselves

What would it mean for our self-perception if we shuffled the traditional hierarchies? What if our perspective on earth changed, that is, if we changed our frame of reference for thinking about ourselves? It became clear in the previous chapters that it would mean taking our earth-centredness as a fixed point within what is, and always will be for us, a physically heliocentric universe. That is another fixed point. For the sun is not only the perceived centre of our solar system. Its energy is central to the support of all life on earth's surface, including ours. Or nearly all. We now know of aphotic living organisms within deep sea vents on the Atlantic Ridge with a unique chemical life-support system that does not depend directly on energy from the sun.

For the rest of us, stating our essential heliocentrism may appear so obvious as to be a point scarcely worth making. Yet accepting its implications would, I believe, initiate a sort of 'velvet revolution' within each of us that runs directly contrary to the kind of self-perception presently taken for granted. Changing our perception of our common relationship to the sun would help change our perception of ourselves in relation to the whole earth community and, by doing so, bring us down to earth through a deepening understanding of that being our proper, indeed our rightful place. It would mean living *as if* we understand and give priority to the complex range of interdependent relationships on which all life here depends and in which we are totally involved.

Vaclav Havel's prototypical 'velvet' revolution (in which one lives in a far from ideal situation 'as if' in an ideal one) suggests that such a change in self-perception can bring about real change. It is true that the need for change in regard to our membership of the earth community is not as evident to us as it was to him when he and some other members of the Czechoslovakian State decided to live as if they were what they later became in fact – Czech Republicans. I am proposing a reverse revolutionary order: looking back through our species' history and seeing ourselves as belonging to a much longer and older ancestry. Then instead of perceiving ourselves as somehow separate from the other members of the earth community, we remember ourselves as part of that larger one and live accordingly. We live *as if* we are what we have always been – members of the community of life on earth.

This velvet revolution chooses certain heliocentric moments in the history of that community – such as the evolution of earth's own body and of the body of life on earth – as our personal frame of reference. This in turn changes our perspective on our internal and external relations with the present community's other members. For we come to see them as not only contributing directly to that community but as essential for our own belonging to any community – whether physical, political, genetic, religious or scientific.

Changing the frame of reference

The expression 'the ground of our being' was used by philosopher and theologian Paul Tillich as a symbol for God and many found it helpful in that respect. But I suggest that before we use it to express the reality of divine presence we need to deepen our meditative awareness of the 'ground of being' beneath our feet. In our urbanized societies the sense of this reality has largely been lost. A lifetime's experience of walking solely on city streets can lead, for many of us, to a total loss of any sense of connection between that experience and being supported by the earth beneath those pavements.

One of the most helpful concepts developed for dealing with this awareness deficit has been that of our 'ecological footprint'. William Rees and his student Mathis Wackernagel coined the phrase not only to quantify the human demand on the earth in terms of the appropriated ecosystem area needed to sustain city life but also because he realized how important it was to bring human dependence on Nature home to his North American students. Many of them, he said, almost by definition come from relatively wealthy and consumerist communities where that dependence appears to have been all but eliminated by human technological progress. Water comes in bottles; milk in cartons: vegetables in plastic wraps and meat in individually wrapped bite-sized chunks (Wackernagel 1996).

It is hardly surprising, then, that in our consumerist culture, awareness of the fact that our food actually comes from earth-supported plants and animals, who themselves rely on the sun's energy to support their lives, is in very short supply. Our perception of this is occluded if not effectively blocked by technological intervention between primary source and human consumer. I will attempt to enlarge that perception in this chapter.

Gaia theory is highly relevant to this enlargement as it helps deepen our understanding of what it means to be a member of the interdependent community of life on earth. It shows how our lives have an earth ancestry as well as a human one; that they depend, in a very real sense, on continuous tight bonding between all life and its physical and chemical environment – and that the presence and strength of that bond depends ultimately on the gift of energy from sun to earth. Sun worshippers before and after Copernicus have recognized this fact and responded to it in different ways. So an important moment in completing the personal Copernican revolution is to see my life, in common with all life on earth, as sun-centred, sun-dependent. And then to live as consciously as possible in the light of this knowledge.

Someone who has clearly discerned and called for this re-visioning of the sun-centred self is Buddhist teacher Thich Nhat Hanh. In the aptly titled *The Sun My Heart* he observes:

> We know that if our heart stops beating, the flow of our life will stop, and so we cherish our heart very much. Yet we do not often take the time to notice that there are other things, outside of our bodies, that are also essential for our survival. Look at the immense light we call the sun. If it stops shining, the flow of our life will also stop, and so the sun is our second heart, our heart outside of our body. This immense 'heart' gives all life on earth the warmth necessary for existence.
>
> (Nhat Hanh 1988: 66f.)

The biological revolution

This sun-centred framework focuses our attention on the simple fact that it is the primary provider of energy for almost all life on earth. Nhat Hanh goes on to draw attention to an accompanying fact: that members of that community, as in all communities, have roles and abilities directly related to their particular kind of body and to the way in which they use their energy. Each of us does more for the community than simply live within it. Plants, for example, contribute to the well-being of all members because their leaves absorb the sun's energy, along with carbon dioxide from the air, to produce food for the tree, the flower, the plankton – and they do this not only for themselves but for those animals (like ourselves) who do not have this ability to photosynthesize. In this way all of us, he says – people, animals and plants – 'consume' the sun, directly and indirectly. This common principle governs all living things and unites them at a very fundamental level of being.

Artist and scientist Glynn Gorick, in a picture entitled *Sunlight Harvesting*, concentrates on its harvesting in the waters of the planet. He depicts the molecular structure of subvisible microscopic marine algae that act like solar panels in their absorption of energy from photons of sunlight. This energy is used by them to turn carbon dioxide and water into food, releasing excess oxygen into the earth's atmosphere. This process began billions of years ago when these algae were among the most advanced life forms on earth. They changed the earth's atmosphere and made it possible for oxygen-breathing animals to evolve – eventually including us.

Reading Nhat Hanh and looking again at Glynn's painting reminded me of a conversation with James Lovelock about the symbolic and functional hierarchies that underlie so many human institutions and determine the distribution and use of power within them. He remarked that the only natural hierarchy in our lives is that which governs our relationship with the sun. This natural hierarchical relationship makes us, in common with all life on earth, dependent on the power of the sun's energy – whether we remember it or not. In contrast to human hierarchies, however, its power over all our lives is exercised impartially. It shines on the just and the unjust: on the tiniest organism and the mightiest tree.

The fact of our common dependence on the sun has led to scientists calculating the years remaining before the sun moves out of the earth's orbit – or burns it up. The calculations are sufficiently well accepted to have given rise to the joke about a planetarium lecturer who tells his audience that in five billion years, the sun will become a bloated red giant that will engulf Mercury, Venus and eventually, earth. Afterwards an anxious member of the audience asks:

> 'Excuse me, Doctor. Did you say that the Sun will burn up the Earth in 5 billion years?'
> 'Yes, more or less.'
> 'Thank God. For a moment I thought you said 5 million.'
>
> (Sagan 1997: 6)

In the meantime, the sun remains the fixed point of reference for our lives. That fact focuses attention on what makes life on earth, in human or any other form, possible. Then, as Nhat Hanh indicated, we may look more deeply into what *on earth* makes our life possible. This leads to a further revolution in self-perception already touched on in regard to marine algae. Technology may now make it possible to go into an oxygen bar in a major city and buy some. But what about those organisms who originally supplied it? And continue to do so. Do we feel we owe them any debt of gratitude?

Just to pose such a question involves what Lewis Thomas calls 'the biologic revolution'. It is, he says, 'a curious, peaceful sort of revolution, in which there is no general apprehension that old views are being outraged and overturned.' He points out that he was raised in the belief that organelles (mitochondria and chloroplasts) were obscure little engines inside his cells, owned and operated by him or his cellular delegates. Now, however, he learns that some of them (and the most important at that) are total strangers to him, since their DNA is qualitatively different from his. He had never bargained on descent from single cells without nuclei. He could even make his peace with that, he says, if it were all. But there is the added humiliation that 'I have not, in a real sense, descended at all. I have brought them all along with me, *or perhaps they have brought me*' (Thomas 1975: 81f. My italics).

Thomas implicitly challenges the idea I have of myself as someone in control of a human body with a purely human ancestry. Instead I begin to see myself as someone descended not only from family lineages but with an 'earth' ancestry continuous with and contingent on the evolution of life on earth. This means realizing that I carry live within my body some of the earliest life forms on earth. And that, in a very real sense, they have carried me along with them to this moment.

I found a useful image of this biological revolution recently on a picture postcard that shows the prototypical ark sailing gracefully over the waves, its decks and windows filled with various happily waving animals, reptiles and birds. From the point of view of our evolution within Gaia, the ark represents the conditions within which life emerged and flourished in diverse forms over billions of years. Its substructure was laid down by and is maintained by oxygen-tolerant and life-sustaining organelles and is held together by their persistent tight coupling with their environments. The energy that carries it and its passengers along comes from the sun that lights up the whole scene. That includes a dinghy full of vigorously rowing humans trying to catch up with the animals' ark.

Late-comers by about three billion years or so, we 'caught up' eventually and have been carried along by the Gaian life community ever since. Our place in the picture illustrates the role reversal that, as Lewis Thomas points out, requires a revolution in the idea we have of ourselves. And of algae, mitochondria and chloroplasts. His understanding of subvisible organisms strongly and consistently interacting with each other and with their environments in order to create the conditions for sustaining life on earth is not, however, usually considered revolutionary – and will not be, until we take it seriously as a reversal in who or what has counted most in earth history and in the drama within it called the emergence and evolution of life. Until we consider their ceaseless labours as a transformative gift in our lives to be met with gratitude and used by us to sustain and re-create life.

One reason Thomas gives for our not taking our biological inheritance/

ancestry seriously is that our knowledge of it has been used simply as an opportunity to make money: rather like the Victorian industrial revolution and the discovery of the power of steam. (See above for oxygen bars.) Staying with the analogy of the ark, this suggests that since we emerged on deck we have assumed that, like Noah, we have been given overall control of it. But over the past 200 years or so this has meant that increasingly we have played a pirate's role – though pirates are not so foolish as to hack vital pieces off their boats and offer them for sale to each other in return for pieces of gold. They would know that their lives depend on the boats. And they would also know that as they (probably) did not build them in the first place, they couldn't re-build them either. Nor could they provide the energy that propelled them and keeps them afloat.

Tom Wakeford is at once more forthright about the biological revolution and more hopeful of it making its proper impact on us now that its nature is becoming better known. Previous concentration on mammals, he says, led to bacteria being seen as primitive beings that long ago passed the torch of evolutionary innovation on to large organisms. Now, however, in spite of personality politics, technological backwardness and blind ignorance, the revolutionary insight that bacteria are the eternal innovators in the history of life is celebrated (by him at least) as one of the greatest breakthroughs in the history of science (Wakeford 2001: 13–15).

Outside science too, if taken seriously and pursued to its logical and practical conclusions, this revolutionary insight subverts the accepted order of things. It overturns the present view of my 'self' as a body belonging to me and to no other – and of myself as isolated by space and time from other life forms. Instead I come to see my existence as connected to and inter-dependent with the community of life on earth over a vast span of time. And to see that throughout that timespan, the reciprocal exchanges of energy between the largest and the smallest bodies, from that between the sun and the earth to that between mammoth and tree, bacteria and me, have intimately concerned me. And they still do. This is the revolution in human self-perception and in our sense of human importance that Gould sees as intrinsically connected to the discovery of 'deep time'. I connect it to that aspect of deep time addressed by Gaia theory: our belonging naturally to the emergence and evolution of organisms and their environment on earth as a single coupled process.

Obstacles to self-revolution

However, there are formidable psychological obstacles to consciously making a transition to being an earth-centred rather than a totally human-centred being. For a start, would I then (as Brecht's cardinal feared) have to see myself as insignificant? To use Lewis Thomas's word, would I be humiliated? Does not my significance as a human being depend on my ability to assert my autonomy, my self-rule, over and against that of other human individuals and all other beings? Or, does my life actually matter to more than those humans touched by it in some way? Furthermore, can my sense of self come from more than my relationships to other human selves?

The difficulty of having these last two proposals adopted as a basis for human selfhood is illustrated in a poster produced by the conservation department of the Council of Europe. It depicts European species entitled to conservation under the Berne Convention and includes the largest possible number in all shapes and sizes from the tiniest snail and insect to the largest mammal. Its title is *Family Portrait*. When I show this to people they exclaim at its beauty and accuracy and the zoologically knowledgeable among them are quick to point out and name species missing from the line-up. To date no one has said: 'We are'!

What we have here is the currently accepted perspective on the ark picture described above. The humans do not, it is assumed, belong among the members of the ark community. They have got a distinctive boat of their own that they can and have used to catch up with the ark. And according to the conventional understanding of the covenant contract with its architect, they then take it over – even if this has meant killing or throwing overboard most of the previous inhabitants.

The humans themselves, however, are assumed to be a uniquely protected species under the terms of that covenant contract. And they have protected that status throughout human history under the guise of other laws, contracts and covenants. Only now is there a slowly growing realization (evident in 'conventions' as to which animals are to be 'conserved' and which can be killed) that this separation of our species from all others in terms of life value has profound effects on our own lives.[7]

The consensus is still strong, however, on our species being exceptionally 'special'; on our having arrived (to stay with the picture postcard ark) from somewhere else and under our own steam. This ensures that more than a hundred years after Darwin we are born into a culture that routinely confines our family membership to human blood relatives or to those legally adopted into a family group. We see ourselves as distanced from and looking on at other living beings: at a distance and with a stance which affects our perspective on them and our understanding of them. We see ourselves as exceptions to the progress of life in general: as outside of the necessary processes and conditions that brought all other forms of life into existence.

So we consistently leave ourselves out of the deep time history of the emergence and evolution of life on earth. Or when we recite that history (as

I have found in some recitations of what is popularly called 'the Universe Story') we finish it with our emergence. There is no intimation that there are chapters yet to come; or that our being here is not the whole point of the narrative. And so, as in the Noah story, it seems that our lives are exceptionally important.

For centuries before Darwin, religious doctrine and philosophical teachings made the case for God (or the gods) granting us this exceptional status. Now, long after his concept of the origin and evolution of all species has gained almost universal recognition outside of some religious fundamentalist sects, it is still the case that the claim to human exceptionalism (on the grounds of our specific mode of consciousness, or of our intellect or of our capacity for language rather than our soul) holds as strong a grasp as ever on our self-perception. Not least because this exceptionalism is enshrined in what Giorgio Agamben calls the biopolitical sphere: the ambiguous zone where the policies and instruments of the state both guard human life and, at the same time, arrogate to themselves the power to kill without being guilty of the crime of murder. It is human life alone however, that is *unquestionably* the sole and worthy subject, and object, of both protection and extinction under the law – conservation conventions notwithstanding.

I mention Agamben because he distinguishes (as, he says, does classical Greek) between life as *zoē* ('bare life' that expresses the simple fact of living common to all living beings) and life as *bios* (the specifically different form or way of living proper to a human individual or group). The difference lies, he says, in a capacity for *logos* (language) that is tied to politics. He cites a pertinent passage from Aristotle's *Politics* that is worth quoting here:

> Among living beings, only man has language. The voice is the sign of pain and pleasure, and this is why it belongs to other living beings. . . . But language is for manifesting the fitting and the unfitting and the just and the unjust. To have the sensation of the good and the bad and of the just and the unjust is what is proper to men as opposed to other living beings. And the community of these things makes dwelling and the city [that is, politics].
>
> (Agamben 1995: 7–8)

This is a telling description of what has happened in the process of human urbanization, defined here as dwelling in a city constituted by human politics that are conducted through language. No one listens to the sound of other than a human voice. No trace of the ecological footprint is observed. Agamben's main discussion is of the ancient figure of the man who may, by law, be killed but not murdered (*homo sacer*). He is the epitome of the distinction between *zoē* ('bare life') and *bios* (that in the human biopolitical community) and its relationship to death. (I shall return to this later.) What is relevant here is the philosophical assumption that politics and law are *only* concerned with human life and that what makes it 'human life' as opposed to 'bare life' is *logos*, defined here in relation to politics simply as 'language'. Implicit in the definition however is the human ability to distinguish between the just and the unjust, the good and the bad (human being) through the exercise of our reason (ibid.: 1–11). And what I want to draw attention to is the fact that this ability has been legally exercised, almost entirely up to now, in respect of human beings alone. In practice, this means that no other 'being' appears to exist within political discourse or to merit the protection of the law.

These basic assumptions about the distinctive nature of our human being has fed into the commonplace, generally accepted perception of the distinctiveness of the human 'self' in its relationships with other living beings. Clearly this self includes our rational and linguistic faculties. But, as we saw with Copernicus, it also includes physical, aesthetic and emotional factors that colour our observations and draw on whatever experience we have of the world through sensory observation and experiment. Both components (rational understanding and experiential learning) are commonly seen as part of our selves. In the previous chapter I showed how both play an essential role in our knowing anything about the earth, or about the universe.

Rational understanding, however, is commonly seen as residing in the mind while experiential, sensual faculties are assumed to be located in the body. Another factor in their relationship emerged in the previous chapter when, as we saw, our ability to reason, while still located in the body, takes us imaginatively to places inaccessible to bodily experience. But it does not get us there or leave us there. Nor do we describe those places in other than bodily terms.[8]

Earth and self

Now another traditional hierarchy (of mind over body) that is an underlying obstacle to my being earth-centred begins to surface. The question of defining the self in relation to earth becomes problematic for men and women alike when (personalized female) 'earth' is seen as the archetypal Cartesian 'body without mind': that is, without rationality. And therefore, we may suppose, without a 'self'. Or, by implication, without self-worth. So how are we to relate to earth? How do we relate to a mindless, that is, presumably 'self-less' body?

One way to find out is to look at the results of denying possession of a self to earth: of denying it its own worth. Remember Rilke's impassioned plea to God to 'hold on to your self-possession!' Otherwise, he reminds us, we may call God (and earth) 'mine!' So if it is assumed (as it generally is) that earth does not possess a self, we may (and do) relate to it merely as a possession: *our* possession; one which enhances our sense of self-worth rather than that of earth itself. We say publicly (as I have seen a talk entitled) that 'the earth belongs to all its people!' This is intended as a call to justice for them all (as indeed it is). And as I mentioned already, when China announced a programme for putting people on the moon and mining its resources it evoked the indignant response from one leader writer: 'The moon belongs to us all!'

But this attitude does no justice to earth or moon. For in fact they belong to no one. And certainly not to us, belonging as we do among earth's youngest progeny. If we trace her life back to its mysterious beginnings we find that her self-possession should be as precious to us, and as sacrosanct, as God's. Or, to stay with the present analogy, as our mother's. Which of us could or would want to say that we 'possess' our mother – in the sense of being granted power to use her body for our own ends?

The prevailing assumption, however, is that while our human mother possesses a self, and therefore cannot be possessed, the earth possesses no 'self'. This assumption surfaced most clearly when James Lovelock presented Gaia as a self-regulating organism. He described that self-regulation in scientific terms: as its ability to take in free energy (either externally sourced, as sunlight, or internally sourced through the earth's crust as chemical potential energy) and use it for its own purposes: as the ability to keep its climate in a dynamic (not unchanging) state of constancy or homeostasis. This ability, he said, defines a living organism. And 'Gaia would be a living organism under the physicist's or the biochemist's definitions' (Lovelock 1991: 29, 141f.).

The term 'regulation' was used by him in a cybernetic sense, as the tendency for a system to counteract perturbation and external forcing. In its broadest sense it is simply a tendency to counteract change. He used the term 'homeostasis' to mean regulation towards a fixed set point. In biology it describes the regulation by an organism of its internal environment in an optimal state for its physiological processes. In the case of Gaia, the regulation is seen as the outcome of tight life–environment coupling, in which organisms both alter and are constrained by their environment (Lenton 2002; Lenton in press).

Lovelock's argument that Gaia is *self*-regulating brought scorn on his head from other scientists, particularly those who, as he said, follow Descartes in distinguishing humans from all other living things in alone possessing a soul. By doing so, Lovelock pointed out, they limit a general property, soul or life, to a specific class of owner, the human person

(Lovelock 1991: 31). One can see here the epistemological privilege of Christianity, reinforced by that of science, working to claim absolute uniqueness, within evolutionary history, for the human soul/mind or self (the anthropic principle again). Both religion and science have successfully established as (supposedly) absolutely true, in all instances and for all time, what is, after all, merely a human assumption: that no other body than the human exercises rationality or mind in order to keep itself in an optimal state either for enjoying or regulating its life properly. And therefore that the human body, which does 'possess', but is not solely a rational mind, alone possesses or is a 'self'.

What follows from this for non-human earthy creatures (as we have seen from the Noah story and its Augustinian and scientific pirate sequels) is that as they are deemed totally earthy/irrational, so they are subject to man. And if this is true of them, how much more must it be true of earth? Or of Gaia? So the possibility of her 'self'-regulating is deemed nonsensical. And as a consequence, the tight coupling between the human self and earth's self, and the kind of intimate relationship this implies, is further weakened. For wherever the body/mind distinction is held to absolutely, there is always at best an implied superiority (and therefore legitimate dominance) attributed to human (male) 'mind'. And as the sense of earth's worth is weakened, the impulse to detach our selves from earth in order to enhance our own worth is further increased. The pirates do not feel they are hacking away at themselves. We are distanced from the bodies in the earth family portrait, according to Aristotle, through our logical power to order and name those within it who do not have this power so to order and name us, or themselves.

Wherever the distinction is held to, or however it is made, what matters is that if absolute priority is granted to mind *or* to body, the distinction functions by elevating or degrading one at the expense of the other. It can be a useful distinction in that we know that we are, mysteriously, more than our bodies (as was demonstrated in the journeyings through the universe mentioned at the beginning of the previous chapter); or, rather less mysteriously, more than our minds – just as Lovelock knows that Gaia is 'more than' the sum of its parts and Rilke knows that God is 'more than' anything we can hold to, speak of, or see. But when the distinction is used divisively, to separate bodies from minds or the physical from the 'metaphysical' in order to exalt the latter and so dismiss, devalue or discount the former, it blocks rather than opens the possibility of a real relationship between my self and earth's self: one in which both my rational and my experiential faculties play a positive and essential role.

I take this to mean that my relationship with the earth is one that exercises all my faculties in different ways and in various combinations. And that it involves consistently relating that personal involvement with earth on my part to the involvement of earth in my life: to its gifting me continuously with what I need to live. One way of doing this is to use my own rational, analytic, 'scientific' faculties to deepen my understanding of earth's self as manifested in its laws and its life forms; its history and the possible direction of its future. But my feelings too are engaged: feelings of wonder, care, empathy, joy and now, all too often, desolation at what is happening to the earth family.

For all that I can point to as 'me', as self, is engaged with and in relationship with earth's self. As ultimately, on a different timescale, all of earth's self is engaged with other bodies in the solar system but primarily with its centre: the sun that through the influence of its gravitational field coalesced cosmic debris of unknown origin into the body we call 'earth' and then made life upon it possible. There is only one earth–ark for me to live in: the one originally constructed by the tight coupling of subvisible organisms and their environment and continuously renovated by them and other life forms over billions of years. The evidence for this is the total engagement over time of all earth's elements in creating and sustaining the atmospheric constants essential for life: now, for my life. Poet Gerard Manley Hopkins says simply: 'The self selves. What I do is me.' What the earth does is what the earth is. It 'earths' life in all its forms, whether bare or clothed in human guise.

Similarly I am not only what I think, or what I feel. I am what I am through dynamic interactions between earth processes that themselves enable me to think and feel and to turn from regarding the earth or any living being on it as simply 'there' for me. Becoming aware of my own self-making, I gradually become aware of earth's self-making. And vice versa. The concept of self-making (*autopoiesis*) was explored at length in *Sacred Gaia*, principally in regard to human self-making – but always on the understanding that it couples me tightly with and contributes to the self-making of earth, or Gaia.

Without that intrinsic connection between myself and earth's self, my significant relationships with other human beings could not occur. Without it, I cease to relate to anything or anyone. This is another way of saying that my self exists because earth's self exists; and that if earth's self did not exist, the self I call mine would not exist. And that if I did not exist, earth's self would still exist. This is where the demand for geocentrism demands a change in self perspective. Priority is not something *I* can bestow on earth. Earth's self simply has, and will always have, physical, temporal and existential priority over mine.

Articulating these realities as clearly as possible enables me to turn towards and to express a commitment to the truth that without earth, there would be no relationships between human selves. There would be no one there to relate to. When we meet a child, even if the parents are not present we know that the child would not be here if they had not already been here. We are so used to this state of affairs that we pay no attention to it. So we ignore or discount earth's history as essential prelude to and part of our history. We disregard the fact that if earth did not exist, we would not exist. We behave now, most of the time, as if we just appeared one day in the earthscape (Primavesi 2000: 9), or (for those of a Platonic persuasion) were placed there from somewhere else *above* earth. For those of no religious or philosophical persuasion, the unthoughtout assumption is, as Rees found when developing the concept of the ecological footprint, that human technology has and does 'create' the environment that supports us.

Within the Christian tradition we have been taught that our ancestors, Adam, or Noah, from whom all of us descended, were placed on earth by God. And that Adam, or man, is distinguished from all other life forms in his God-given power to 'name' the other creatures – an ability that Carl Linnaeus, one of its greatest exponents, considered a divinely conferred human task. And that our (biopolitical) lives alone are sacrosanct because we were formed in God's image. And furthermore, that we have been given power of life and death over all other creatures.

In a secularized society this perception of ourselves is more likely to be articulated in terms of Platonic categories of divine Mind residing in the Empyrean and creating 'minds' which, once embodied on earth may, after a period of trial there, return to the Empyrean as disembodied minds. This self-perception, subconsciously at least, gives plausibility to the many popular fictions in which we come and go from or to other planets. And our desire to distinguish ourselves absolutely from earth and to see our-selves as having a singular destiny (on a destination other than earth) makes those fictions welcome.

A shift in perception

Therefore to make a conscious transition from such perceptions of myself to a perception of my being an earth-centred human, I need to relate to earth *as if* my whole existence depends on that relationship. I need to relate to my fellow human beings *as if* our earth lineage were as central to our being alive as are our human genealogies. I need to relate to them *as if* their earth-centredness is as essential for my being with them and their being with me as are their human parents. I say *as if* because we need to grow into this kind of attention to our earth heritage. It does not come naturally to us (in one sense) to regard that heritage as what it is: Gaia's gift handed to us by countless unknown beings throughout their lives – or passed on to us at the moment of their death.

Yet as Thich Nhat Hanh reminds us, this becomes a reality every time we eat. Here is a version of this truth offered as part of a Eucharistic celebration:

From air and soil
From bees and sun,
From others' toil
My bread is won.

And when I bite
The soil, the air,
The bees and light,
Are still all there.

So I must think
Each day afresh
How food and drink
Became my flesh.

And then I'll see
The air, the sun,
The earth, the bee
And me, all one.
(As quoted in Primavesi 2000: 161)

Scientifically I may trace my earth lineage back through billions of years throughout which different levels of calcium, oxygen, silicon, or potassium emerged, merged and then, after interacting with other elements, provided the physical material which would one day constitute my bone structure (Levi 1985: 224–233). I can walk by the sea and the sand beneath my feet contains skeletal remains of algae which lived thousands of millions of years ago in the depths of the ocean and drew down sulphur and carbon out of the atmosphere and so kept the fresh-water cycle flowing which provides me with the drink I need at the end of my walk.

I can lie in a field and dream of the time, between one and two million years ago, when an ancestor moved out of the ancient forest and made a new life on the grassy plain. She responded, some anthropologists think, to the unspoken demand of grass, by moving for the first time in human history in a long loping stride across the open savannah. I may rest my head on a tussock of *caespitose* grass that builds long-running dynasties remaining close to their place of origin through a method which Graham Harvey calls 'securing immortality'. Instead of forming a turf, new 'families' of tillers develop inside the encompassing leaves of the established plant and under this protection put down their own roots. Eventually (after sixty years or so) they form a new generation of plants clustered around the parent. And as the 'family group' expands, so the diameter of the tussock on which my head rests has slowly increased to where it now accommodates me comfortably (Harvey 2001: 10f., 92f.).

In all such moments of awareness I am living and experiencing the scientific truth that evolution connotes 'change' over time rather than human centred 'progress'. As I do this I move from viewing my life solely in terms of contemporary human societies or individuals 'making' progress and thereby earning respect and acquiring significance. Are they more significant to me than the human being who first loped across the savannah, and if so, why? For *'how recently an organism evolved does not define its "worth"'* (Liebes 1998: 8. My italics).

Perhaps now we get a glimpse of how 'revolutionary' it is to see earth as the centre of my life: to see it as the hub around which the wheel of my life, and all life on earth, revolves. The extraordinary thing is, of course, that it should require a 'revolution' for me to see myself as what in fact I am: an earthling related to other species and to all our forebears back to a single cell. Up to now I have related to myself (and to others) as a 'self' made up of a human body and mind that relates solely to other human selves who are similarly constructed. Sometimes I relate to them more through my body than with my mind, or vice versa. But I have been blind to the fact that I and all those humans I am related to, as family or as friends or nations, would not exist if earth did not exist: if they were not primarily related to earth, in every sense and with every sense.

To cope with this form of earth-blindness, I need to live consciously *as if* I am earth-centred. That is, I have to shift my sense of what is significant solely from what humans have accomplished in their lifetime to what earth has accomplished and is accomplishing throughout its existence. And that means living *as if* earth and *all* that belongs to earth (not just to us) is significant.

This does not mean (I am speaking here to myself) button-holing other people about being earth-centred, or violently denouncing those who evidently are not. There is an analogy here with other 'velvet' revolutions which I have found very helpful. Christopher Hitchens draws attention to their character when he says that in the interval between 1968 and 1989, when many of the revolutionaries against consumer capitalism metamorphosed into human rights activists, there were long periods when nothing much seemed to happen. In order to survive those years of stalemate a number of important dissidents evolved a strategy for survival. 'In a phrase, they decided to live "as if"' – as if things were the way they ought to be (Hitchens, *Guardian* 10 November 2001: 3).

Vaclav Havel, for instance, realized that 'resistance' in its original insurgent and militant sense was then impossible in central Europe. He therefore proposed living 'as if' he were a citizen of a free society; 'as if' lying and cowardice were not mandatory patriotic duties; 'as if' his government had signed (which it actually had) the various treaties and agreements that enshrine universal human rights. At around the same time, and alarmed in a different way by many of the same things, Professor E.P. Thompson proposed that we live 'as if' a free and independent Europe already existed. In the deep south in the 1960s Rosa Parks decided to act 'as if' a hardworking black woman could sit down on a bus at the end of a day's labour (ibid).

Hitchens warns his readers that this is not easy, as they may well be confronted with some species of bullying or bigotry or appeal to the general will. Everybody needs tactics, and he advises us ironically to try behaving 'as if' these responses need not be tolerated and are not inevitable.

So at present, when we are being informed by an increasing number of experts that our well-being is bound ineluctably to the well-being of all living beings on earth, while at the same time we are urged to live as though it depends solely on whether or not human consumerist demands on earth are met, it makes sense to live 'as if' our lives are earth-centred. In other words, to live *as if* earth is what in fact it is: the ground of my being. *As if* everything I am and everything I have is, ultimately, what it is: earth's gift to me. *As if* my self-regulation is intimately connected, in all its aspects, with the self-regulation of Gaia; with her ability to maintain optimal conditions for the physiological processes which sustain all life. Which is indeed the case.

This velvet revolution, like all the others, frees us to be what in fact each of us is: a person with human rights; a tired black woman sitting comfortably on a bus; an earth-centred human self which is not simply a passenger or pirate on the ark of life but a vital member of it: one dependent on reciprocal exchanges with all its physical and chemical component parts. They bind the sun and me, the earth and I, the I and the not-I together.

Deep and deeper into time

Part of the problem here is that our self-making works on a very different timescale to that of earth's. Our short lives leave little time for getting to know such an ancient living entity as Gaia who does not personally address us. Tolkien helps us imagine what might happen if she did. He describes an encounter between short-lived hobbits and what is still the oldest living creature on the surface of the planet, a giant tree. Treebeard, as he names himself, is puzzled by the appearance of these new creatures since, he says, he cannot find their names in the lists of living creatures he learnt when he was young. He knows who, or what he is: 'Ent, the earthborn, old as mountains.' Hobbits, however, are not on any of his lists. He agrees to include them although, as he says, they are inclined to be rather hasty and do not seem to fit in anywhere. He knows, however, that his and their destinies coincide (Tolkien 1968: 485f.).

Here, for me at least, lies part of the answer to the question of our significance. To whom or to what are we significant? Our lives are significant, ultimately, to every living being now and in the future. They do and will depend on Gaia's ability to self-regulate earth's temperatures within a range comfortable for human life. Just as the lives of those who have lived before us were significant contributors to our present comfort or discomfort. George Eliot puts it magnificently when she says at the end of *Middlemarch* that the fact 'that things are not so ill with you and me as they might have been, is half owing to the number who lived faithfully a hidden life, and rest in unnumbered tombs'. I would want to extend my gratitude not only to them but to all the unnamed and unnoticed life forms who lived and worked faithfully and ceaselessly within Gaia throughout her evolution and my own. They have made my life not only 'not so ill', but possible.

In the same way the progress of my own self-making and its inputs to my *SocialScape* (Primavesi 2000: 8), now or later, affect the present and future *EarthScape* of all living beings (ibid.: 91–92). The revolution within my self that I am groping towards turns me *towards* a consciousness of this: of my self as a participant in the earth's life, and of the earth as a participant in my life. In Thomas Berry's illuminating phrase, being conscious that 'earth acts in all that acts upon the earth' (Berry 1990: 153). So I change to acting 'as if' earth acts in me. 'As if' my self-making is intrinsically dependent on and tightly coupled with that of earth. 'As if' my self-worth is not worth more than that of earth. And the more counter-cultural that idea of ourselves and of earth appears to be, the more we need to live as if it is true. Because it is.

So poet Wallace Stevens writes in *The Planet on the Table*:

> His self and the sun were one
> And his poems, although makings of his self,
> Were no less makings of the sun.
>
> It was not important that they survive.
> What mattered was that they should bear
> Some lineament or character,
>
> Some affluence, if only half perceived
> In the poverty of their words,
> Of the planet of which they were part.
> (Stevens 2000: 532)*

*From *The Collected Poems of Wallace Stevens* by Wallace Stevens, copyright 1954 by Wallace Stevens and renewed 1982 by Holly Stevens. Used by permission of Alfred A. Knopf, a division of Random House, Inc./Faber and Faber Ltd.

6 Heaven on earth

Implicit in the previous chapters is the religious notion that the astronomical 'heavens' above the earth observed and described by Copernicus were the visible indicator of a theological 'heaven' beyond them: one in which God dwells. While the present Hubble perspective on the universe takes us far beyond that of Copernicus, it is still the case that 'heaven', understood as a place beyond the visible universe, inhabited by God, plays an important role in religious discourse and in western cultural imagination generally.

What kind of role? In one of his most famous songs, John Lennon exhorted us to 'imagine there's no heaven', telling us that 'it's easy if you try'. But why should we try? What would result from our '*un*imagining' heaven? We would, he thought, then be able to imagine earth without a hell below it while above it, there would be 'only sky'. This vision of earth would, he hoped, positively affect our lives. It would enable us to live in the present; to do away with geographical and national boundaries; to live without religion; to give up our possessions and to realize that our greed ensures that someone, somewhere, suffers hunger. Above all, we would stop killing each other and live in peace. All this would happen if we used our imagination – to imagine 'there's no heaven'.

But is it really that simple? Lennon keys in here to a common criticism of the religious concept of heaven: that it encourages us to shirk taking effective action to bring about a better world in the present by offering an irrational and illusory escape into a future fantasy one. I shall come back to this criticism. Staying with his lyric, I discern in it a seemingly simpler criticism of heaven that is of particular concern if we are to live an earth-centred life. He reminds us that by imagining life in heaven as the inverse of life on earth, or, rather more exactly, as the inverse of our worst experience of living here, any move to improve it here and now may seem futile, worthless, or redundant. So, he says, get rid of the image of heaven. For as that better life seems postponed indefinitely to a time and place beyond the present, what we do and accomplish here and now seems less and less important. As does the place where we try to accomplish it: earth.

The element of wish-fulfilment in this process, of the wish to have our longing for a better and happier life fulfilled elsewhere in the future, has not, as I said, gone unnoticed. Indeed religion's role in consciously encouraging that process has incurred much more trenchant criticism than Lennon's. Many commentators, from David Hume to Freud and Marx, accuse religions of playing on, indeed fostering the natural desire to escape from present anxieties and intractable problems when they offer the concept of heaven as comfort in present trials.

Anthropologist Stewart Guthrie points out, however, that there are religions without beliefs in an afterlife as well as some who are less than sanguine about this imaginary world. Many have wrathful and capricious deities or semi-divine figures which may perpetuate fears and anxiety rather than allay them. John Ruskin, for example, as the child of Evangelical Anglican parents, lived in a world where 'Damnation awaited most and Death waited for all; a world penetrated by the gaze of an immanent, punishing God who let few escape the pain and horror of hell.' This surely counts as an image of a wrathful and capricious deity. No wish-fulfilment there. Except, perhaps, a rather perverted although perfectly understandable wish to have such horrors visited on others rather than on oneself. Similarly Hume grew up among 'beliefs and practices of great severity and bleakness'. Such views of the afterlife certainly threaten as much as they promise. By doing so, they not only undermine the simplistic version of the wish-fulfilment theory but also demonstrate the complexity and diversity of beliefs about life after death. They express, in a variety of voices, an extraordinary range of viewpoints: using metaphors, symbols and images that, as we shall see, are open to various interpretations.

In his comprehensive study, *The Rise and Fall of the Afterlife*, Jan Bremmer makes the point that the ancient Greeks were traditionally much less concerned with personal survival after death than with social survival in the group. However in the course of the Archaic age this attitude started to change and interest arose in personal survival (Bremmer 2002: 25). Differing Christian perspectives on the afterlife, roughly classifiable as either God-focused or human-focused, emerged in various historic contexts and have been coloured by them. The God-focused perspective is found in the New Testament, where Christians are called on to leave their kin to become 'children of God' here and in the world to come. The human-focused perspective appears in those visions of heaven found in a socially established Christianity where an idealized version of personal relationships continues. In a Gallup poll in 1982, 71 per cent of Americans answered 'yes' to the question: 'Do you think there is a heaven where people who live good lives are eternally rewarded?' What kind of heaven, however, or who would go there, is another matter. The range of possible views on the subject that has emerged over time belies any single assessment of their origin – such as wish-fulfilment (McDannell 2001: 307, 353–357).

The undoubted force of the wish-fulfilment criticism reminds us, however, that what matters is how those interpretative visions of an afterlife are used here and now. They have, and always have had, a latent function in the life of those who hold them. They may function positively, when, as in the case of religious martyrs, they inspire them with courage in the face of state persecution or death. More usually they inspire individuals with hope and commitment to bringing about change in desperate situations of poverty, disease and neglect. Positively and compassionately understood or expressed, some vision of heaven may offer comfort when needed and inspire courage. It can also, however, be used to coerce others into a particular kind of behaviour or to reinforce the epistemological privilege of those who make access to heaven conditional upon acceptance of their authority.

Some of these important issues are thoroughly discussed in the books referenced in this chapter. My overriding concern is to show how the image of heaven in Christian cosmography and cosmology has functioned in relation to our image of earth. Christianity has, as we have seen, exalted heaven at earth's expense, literally, figuratively and symbolically. This has meant that by consistently valuing eternal life after death (in heaven with God) above life on earth, eternal life is made the goal of life on earth. And as a corollary to that, our life here, and that of other living beings, is systematically downgraded. Earth itself, and an earth-centred life, appear not to matter in themselves. They matter only as a means to our achieving what is perceived as our proper destiny: life with God in heaven.

Death and heaven

There are, then, two naturally linked elements in the concept of heaven of particular relevance to an earth-centred life. They are our attitude to death and what we imagine happens to us after it. It is generally accepted by those who believe in heaven that the only way into it is through the gates of death. The hope for heavenly life beyond death can help ameliorate the harsh realities of dying, not only for the person undergoing death but for those left on this side of the gates. And as each of us must venture through them alone, and none return to tell us what lies beyond them, we naturally (not irrationally) try to deal with this reality as best we can.

One of the most common reactions is to insist that death is not the end of our existence:

Us the most fleeting of all.
Just once,
Everything, only for once. Once and no more.
And we, too,
Once. And never Again. But this
Having been once, though only once,
Having been once on earth – can it ever be
Cancelled?

(Rilke 1961: 67)

If, asks Rilke, we have once been on earth, can that 'being' ever be cancelled? Ended? To those of a sanguine religious bent, it is comforting indeed to be told that it may continue happily in heaven. However, in western culture generally, to accept this has meant assuming that there is an immortal, undying part of us, the soul, that lives on there forever. Philo, an Alexandrian Jew of the first century CE whose writings were an attempt to reconcile Greek philosophy with Judaism, greatly influenced early Christian writers in their attempts to do the same for Christian theology. Philo described the 'earthly' man [sic] as one 'moulded' out of the substance of the earth by God; one who is not God's offspring; whose 'earth-like mind ... is corruptible, were not God to breathe into it a power of real life.' When God does so, 'it does not undergo any more moulding [or corruption] but becomes a soul' (Perkins 1994: 210).[9]

The identification of earthiness with mortality and corruption and 'heavenly soul' with immortality became an important one (as we saw in Augustine) for maintaining the essential distinction between man as 'God's offspring' and all other 'earthy' creatures. It remained influential in later Christian attitudes to earthly death and to what, it is hoped, lies beyond it: the soul's final destiny in Paradise. Dante describes that as the place where 'all that dies and all that cannot die', all that is human and all that is divine, are united at last forever. Who would not wish to believe in this heaven?

Using the language of heaven to make our world 'transparent', so that we may glimpse where death takes us, is a proper human response to those moments (such as the death of a loved one) when the world seems most opaque. For who can actually see beyond death? Expressing the 'transparency' of the world at times when our experience of life brings us up sharply and poignantly against its opaqueness, becomes problematic, however, when 'earth' is no longer seen as encompassing or encompassed by 'heaven' but is radically distinguished from it.

The basic theological distinction on which this view of earth and heaven rests is the one between God's presence there (in heaven) and God's absence here (on earth). Earth then ceases to have its own value and its physical configurations – sky, sunlight, mountains, gardens, calm seas, and so on – are valued only in so far as they symbolically correspond to the transcendent ones allotted to heaven. Earth's significance no longer lies in what it is as a whole, in its own total and diffuse reality, but in whatever part of it is used to signify heavenly reality – which lies elsewhere. This is in spite of our believing that, by definition, God is everywhere.

There is another and in some ways equally important element in the Christian attitude to death that has influenced not only our image of heaven but of ourselves in relation to all life on earth. This is the belief that death is not natural for us. While not usually as plainly stated as it is here or as it was by Augustine, this notion has long influenced our attitudes to death. The unstated desire to prove its truth has, unconsciously for the most part, driven and financed many research programmes in how to prolong human life. And as life expectancy rises in affluent societies, so does the expectation that our lifespan can indeed be indefinitely prolonged.

The reasons given by Augustine for saying that death is not natural for us may no longer seem to hold true. But these reasons, and the objections raised against him at the time, are still worth looking at for what they disclose about our self-perception, then and now.

Unnatural death?

Death, said Augustine, is a punishment meted out by God to all living creatures because the first man, Adam, sinned. The 'firstness' of Adam is a cornerstone of much Christian (and now even supposedly post-Christian) thinking. It was raised into prominence, as we saw, in the seventeenth century, when Isaac de La Peyrère was condemned for questioning the existence of this putative individual. The condemnation becomes more understandable (although still not excusable) when considered in the light of the prevailing Augustinian doctrine that Christ redeemed us from the punishment of death meted out to Adam. If Adam, then death. If Christ, then eternal life. It is true that Augustine was not the first to hold the view that Adam's sin brought death to Adam himself. The Gospel of Thomas, which Augustine may or may not have known, says: 'Adam came from great power and great wealth, but he was not worthy of you [or of God, or of heaven]. For had he been worthy he would not have tasted death' (Gospel of Thomas 85). However, the author of this Gospel, unlike Augustine, does not expand on this statement nor draw doctrinal conclusions from it.

During Augustine's lifetime, however, certain Christians influenced by Greek science and philosophy argued (against him) that humanity neither brought death on itself nor could it overcome death by an act of will. Death was in the nature of things. He not only vehemently rejected this view but persuaded Pope Innocent I to condemn those who held it and to excommunicate their leader, Pelagius. This papal condemnation was reversed by Innocent's successor, Zosimus. Augustine then appealed to the secular authorities and secured an imperial condemnation by the Emperor Honorius with which Zosimus was compelled to comply. So Pelagius was again excommunicated by the Pope and condemned to exile by the Emperor (Pagels 1990: 128–133; Noble 1992: 70f.).

This early example of religious coercion used to enforce acceptance of one belief over another foreshadows that exercised against Galileo over a thousand years later. Unlike Galileo, however, Pelagius's view did not ultimately prevail. Augustine's view remains the official one for many Christians today, as anyone who has been to a traditional Christian funeral service will know. Others, too, who have never heard of either Pelagius or Augustine are happy enough, as we shall see, to build on the Augustinian premise that we as a species are in some way an exception to the rules governing all other forms of life on earth. Including the rule that, without death, there is no life.

But I am getting ahead of myself here. Going back to Augustine, for him Adam's 'original sin', the single act of a single human being, '*did* change the structure of the universe itself' by introducing death into it (Pagels 1990: 128–133). (A similar claim for the structural impact of human sin on earth's physical formation was made by Thomas Burnet.) Julian of Eclanum, the most energetic of Pelagius's followers, regarded this view as an enormous error and refused to yield to its superior ecclesiastical and political force. For Julian believed that God gives every human being what he gave Adam – the power to choose one's own moral destiny. And in regard to the universe, he would not accept that its structure was changed by God because one single person sinned. I make the point elsewhere that the word 'sin' is first used in Chapter 4 of the Genesis narrative to describe the murder of Abel by Cain (Primavesi 1991: 223).

Augustine used his interpretation of the opening chapters of Genesis to argue that the universe's structure had indeed been so changed by contrasting actual human experience – of death and pain – with the biblical image of Eden. This was human life as he believed it 'ought to be'. Women ought to experience painless childbearing and enjoy marriage without oppression or coercion. As opposed to what actually happens: they suffer nausea and pain in pregnancy and then greater agonies in childbirth or miscarriage. These, he said, are not *natural*. Nor are men naturally disposed to labour until they sweat (Pagels 1990: 128–133).[10]

Some pertinent aspects of this long debate between Augustine and Julian (it went on for twelve years) emerge from the detailed account of it given by Elaine Pagels. The first is the emphasis Augustine places on the power attributed to one human being, Adam, the prototypical male individual whose actions had deadly consequences 'for the structure of the universe'. Noah was credited with the same pivotal role – although he played the hero's part and redressed the universal consequences of God's punishment of human sin. For Christians he foreshadows Christ, the one who will again decisively change the structure of the universe by his victory over sin and death, 'the last enemy'. Those of Christ's followers who merit that victory shall, we are told, enjoy eternal life in the world to come.

Second, Augustine 'imagines' heaven (on the basis of the Genesis narrative) in contrast to what actually happens on earth. He then uses this imaginative reconstruction to argue for heaven being our natural home. Before we can live there, however, here on earth we are condemned to suffer death, together with the necessity of hard labour to feed ourselves and the attendant sufferings of childbirth. If accepted as true, this view of life on earth as a totally punitive experience adds a particular element to it that has, understandably perhaps, helped to devalue earth in our imaginations.

Earth's image was, of course, even further degraded by its cosmographical association with hell, a place where, for those who do not repent of it, punishment for sin continues forever. This is the hell of eternal damnation somewhere 'below us' that so haunted Lennon's imagination. The lowest circle of Dante's hell, too (where Lucifer is embedded in ice), is located at the lowest and narrowest point of the universe and the one furthest from God (Altcappenberg 2000: 128–131). So while on earth's surface we suffer pain, labour and death, in earth's depths we may suffer eternally the worst physical and spiritual torture: at the furthest possible distance from God in heaven. At best, then, earth is imagined as a transit camp we should leave as soon as possible for our real home in heaven. Or as an examination hall – with hell as a purpose-built, basement punishment block for those who fail to make the grade. One supposedly built, we should note, by a God who also sets and marks the examination papers.

As I write, I am aware that many Christian readers will object to parts of the above summary as unrepresentative of what they believe. However, there will be few who do not recognize some parts as familiar elements of what they were taught (and may still want to believe) about themselves, about the earth and about God. The theological framework within which certain parts fit and function together may now be hidden – but is no less important for that. Turn on a tap and the amount of water we require comes out courtesy of a plumbing system that we cannot see – even one rusty with age and low maintenance.[11]

The third point I want to highlight in this Augustinian dispute is a positive one: Julian's insistence that each of us can *choose* our moral destiny. We are not, after Adam, all destined for hell. Any more than we are all, after

Christ, destined for heaven. Or more exactly, *pre*destined because one individual chose to do wrong, or another chose to die for us. Julian refused to accept that either our physical or our moral destiny was finally determined by the life or activity of anyone other than ourselves. Each of us, he said, works out our destiny in our own time and place, influenced, of course, by those around us, but ultimately responsible for the choices we make. In that sense too, I would say, heaven is here, and now, for us.

The fourth point, allied to that, is the rather obvious one that no single individual has the power to determine the destiny of everyone else – let alone that of the whole universe – for ill or for good. Augustine used his quite extensive power (as we saw in the case of Pelagius) to determine, as he saw it, the correct view of that destiny and so determine it at one remove. Ultimately, however, his power too was limited by that of other thinkers and by the expansion of alternative cultural, religious, scientific and political influences in Europe. La Peyrère stands representative of them.

Pagels sums up the debate's importance by making my fifth point: by now a familiar one but no less important for that. If, she says, Julian's rebuttal of Augustine looks simple – merely common sense – that simplicity is deceptive:

> In fact, *it presupposes a Copernican revolution in religious perspective.* That we suffer and die does not mean that we participate in guilt – neither Adam's guilt nor our own. That we suffer and die shows only that we are, by nature (and indeed, Julian would add, by divine intent), mortal beings, simply one living species among others. . . . *Like Copernicus's revolution, Julian's threatens to dislodge humanity, psychologically and spiritually, from the center of the universe, reducing it to one natural species among others.* He rejects Augustine's primary assumption that Adam's sin transformed nature. To claim that a single human will ever possessed such power reflects a presumption of supernatural human importance.
>
> (Pagels 1990: 144. My italics)

While (for reasons given in previous chapters) I would not agree that Copernicus's revolution really threatened to reduce us to one natural species among others, I agree absolutely that Augustine's claim reflects a presumption of supernatural human importance. That in itself would be enough to give it an overwhelming appeal to those in positions of power. Pagels takes that for granted and looks for other reasons as to why Augustine's view prevailed. One reason she offers is that interpreting suffering as the result of sin or wrongdoing on our part is a persistent, indeed proper human tendency, one by no means limited to Christianity. For we do cause suffering by our actions, sometimes intentionally. Jewish tradition has interpreted personal tragedy similarly. And religions far from both Judaism and Christianity (she cites examples from a Hopi Indian family and from the Azande tribespeople) often express similar assumptions and seek similar explanations. She remarks that Jesus challenged the same assumption among his fellow Jews in regard to the disaster of the tower of Siloam falling and killing eighteen people. 'Do you think', he asked, 'that they were worse than any of the people living in Jerusalem?' (Luke 13:3–5). But Jesus's dissent was an anomaly. 'The overwhelming weight of traditional Jewish and Christian teaching – and perhaps a human tendency to accept personal blame for suffering – implies that suffering and death are the wages of sin' (Pagels 1990: 145–146).

Claiming immortality

It is perhaps understandable, then, to want to lay sin, and the introduction of death into the universe as its punishment, at the door of a mythical ancestor. But Julian alerts us to what we are doing when we go along with this. We are claiming for ourselves the most fundamental exemption clause of all from the laws governing the evolution of life on the planet. The Augustinian claim to our exemption is made in theological terms, that is, that it was written into (evolutionary) history for us by God. But why make it? Latent in that claim is the one Pagels discerns: that God did this because we are of 'supernatural' importance – to God. All of which, after Copernicus, has a very familiar ring indeed.

Latent too is a further pertinent claim: that after death we are completely dissociated from earthly life, hopefully in our enjoyment of eternal life in heaven or, sadly, our suffering it in hell. The theological assumption behind this is that our proper destiny (in every sense) is to live forever: but, ideally, not on earth. The ideal is to dwell with God in heaven for all eternity. Destiny and destination coincide most triumphantly there.

Both assumptions (which is what they are), when examined more closely, reveal a rather more startling presumption that may now be stated as baldly as possible. This is that earth is simply not good enough for us: that we are philosophically (by virtue of our intellects/souls) or theologically (by virtue of our being made in the image of God) destined for somewhere better. When we imagine that better place we call it heaven. A theological corollary to this is the assumption that if earth is not good enough for us, it is certainly not good enough for God. So that 'better' place we call heaven is better, finally, because God dwells there, and not, we may assume, on earth. A purely God-focused heaven ultimately discounts earth as our natural home on the basis that God is not found here. 'The things they think important are earthly things. For us, our homeland is in heaven' (Philippians 3:19); 'Our ancestors recognized that they were strangers and nomads on earth ... they were longing for their heavenly homeland' (Hebrews 11:13–16).

A glance back at the previous chapter shows how antithetical this is to our living 'as if' earth alone is our home and what is entailed in such living. In a statement which brings together a lot of what has been said already about our self-perception, theologian Anna Peterson remarks: 'The human soul and narratives about it bring together creation and salvation in Christian theological anthropology. In the end, the image of God implanted in the human creature returns to God. This means, crucially, that humanity's *real home* does not lie among the rest of creation but rather with God in heaven (Peterson 2001: 30. My italics).

Following through on this logic we find it segues effortlessly into theological claims about our destiny made, so to speak, on God's behalf. It is necessary to remind ourselves at this point that as God did not make earth the centre of the universe, neither did God choose to make what we call hell the lowest point on earth, and earth the most inferior among the heavenly bodies. We did. Nor did God decide, after Adam sinned, not only to discontinue their evening walks but to move residence permanently from earth. We decided that as hell's place, it was no place for God. Nor did God decide that the actions of one human being could change the structure of the universe. Augustine decided that, and many of those alive then and who are alive now have agreed with him for reasons which need to be unwrapped from their canonical bindings.

We may start with the hidden function of the story – what it does to make us exceptional, individually and as a species. That generally remains hidden behind the storm cloud of guilt generated by Augustine's eloquence. That cloud enlarges with every individual's recognition of falling below the highest moral standards that we (as a species) must reach, we are taught, to make us fit for heaven. 'You must therefore be perfect as your heavenly Father is perfect' (Matthew 5:48). Behind the guilt-flecked cloud, therefore, lurks the proud logic of our exceptionalism that presumes we alone are, by nature, capable of being divinely perfect: perfectly fit for heaven.

So countless revisions of and variations on the Flood narrative rely on and at the same time support the central claim that our activities (in the person of the representative man, Adam, or Noah, or Christ) are the catalyst for what happens to all life on earth. This claim may now be judged true in so far as our activities can now be seen to have had increasingly unfortunate consequences for life on earth, if not in the archetypal flood then in unprecedented species extinction, climate change and desertification. But in an Augustinian scenario, this destructive pattern of behaviour wreaks havoc for other species but not, finally, for our own. For we have the ultimate get-out clause: the option of leaving earth to live in heaven with God for all eternity.

This clause, as written and generally interpreted, excludes all other species from the possibility of going on to heaven from earth after death. This has long bothered many thoughtful Christians. The belief that Christ redeemed his chosen followers from death and hell, while satisfying their own most basic personal concern in the face of death, leaves them vaguely or acutely uncomfortable when they realize what it might mean for non-Christians, never mind all other living beings. In the story told of the two thieves who die with Jesus the one who is *not* promised Paradise hangs there representative of the *un*redeemed: both human and non-human. Our proper unease in this regard often points to a subliminal acceptance of Augustinian logic even as its conclusions make us uneasy. So I was once asked when commenting on the Noah story: 'Did Christ justify [or save, or redeem] the rest of creation [that is, the non-human beings]?' To which I replied: 'Why do you think they need justifying?'

Once we question the way the problem is posed, however, our exceptional claim to be destined for heaven appears rather differently. It appears as a clear statement about what we regard as our own status relative to that of all other species: about the supreme status attached to our being the centre and crown of creation. It is a statement made on behalf of God by men who claim the right to make claims on God's behalf. As I pointed out earlier, and it is worth repeating here, more than 1,500 years after Augustine cardinals at the Second Vatican Council proclaimed that 'all things on earth should be related to man [sic] as their centre and crown ... having been created in the image of God ... [man] was appointed by Him [sic] as master of all earthly creatures that he might subdue them and use them to God's glory ... [for] man [sic] is *the only creature on earth which God willed for itself*' (Abbott 1966: 210f., 223. My italics).

The kind of theological language used here to assert our exceptional status, at a time when the theory of Darwinian evolution is generally accepted, tells us a lot not about what we are, but about what we have imagined ourselves to be: *the only creature on earth which God willed for itself*. The only creature, that is, that God considered worth making for its own sake; for its intrinsic worth. Creatures of such worth that the actions of one of them could affect the structure of the universe. Publicly we are more likely now to claim this exceptional status on the scientific authority behind the anthropic principle. Or on that which implies that our destiny is to colonize the universe and, perhaps, again through the power of human intelligence, prolong our lives indefinitely on reaching our preferred destination there. Or on the scientific evidence which shows that our evolution differentiates us from all other animals in that we can reflect on that difference. And furthermore, that we alone can discuss it because of our capacity for symbolic reasoning and articulate speech (Tattersall 1998: 216–235).

All of which belongs to what Peterson calls 'the claim to human exceptionalism in western tradition'. While its Augustinian theological foundations may no longer be visible, they are no less solid for being hidden, surfacing as and when required. Their history raises the question of how much longer we can continue to claim exceptional status. For, apart from its high feel-good factor, one must take account of its *effects*. And those now visible on earth should surely cause us concern. My immediate concern is that if the claim is legitimated as 'theologically' true, then we are claiming that God legitimates the effects of our behaving in an exceptionally supremacist fashion: 'as *master* of all earthly creatures'; rather than as a particular member of the community of life on earth – and nowhere else.

Lest we forget, one reason for negative reactions to Gaia theory is precisely this: that it radically questions this claim to exceptionalism within evolutionary history and so raises fears about the loss of human significance based on that claim. For what greater significance could we give ourselves than that of being an exception to that history? The challenge to this view of ourselves, barely discerned but coming into view after Copernicus, is out in the open now in the implications of Lovelock's work on the evolution of the planetary conditions that made and make human life possible.

Stephen Jay Gould put some of these implications well when he remarked on how comforting and convenient for human domination is the traditional concept of a young earth, ruled by human will within days of its origin. How threatening, by contrast, the notion of human habitation emerging after an almost incomprehensible immensity (of time), just a millisecond before the present by comparison (Gould 1987: 1f.).

Heaven on earth

Forgoing the creationist concept of a young earth threatens the notion that we have a right to dominate it. Or to imagine it as a temporary, second-rate human residence, a staging post on the way to our real home in heaven. Changing one part of that view inevitably affects other parts and, over time, effects a revolution in our perception of who the earth is *for*. We can no longer assume that our emergence is the purpose behind its creation. Then we may find it possible to regard the earth with the joy and largeness of vision displayed by Thomas Hardy:

> Let me enjoy the earth no less
> Because the all-enacting Might
> That fashioned forth its loveliness
> Had other aims than my delight.
> (Hardy 1978: 94)

The exemption clause works the other way round for Hardy. Far from claiming that earth was fashioned 'for us', Hardy assumes the exact opposite. We may have been excluded altogether from the original groundplan! This dramatic shift in self-perception enables us to enjoy earth's loveliness now as gift. We may not claim it as our due nor value it only for its usefulness to us: as something we can possess and exploit for our sole benefit. It is given: neither earned, bought nor expected.

Just as Hardy's opening verse shifts our perspective on earth by questioning who it might have been fashioned for, he concludes the poem with a conjecture that shifts our perspective on heaven too:

> And some day hence, toward Paradise
> And all its blest – if such there be –
> I will lift glad, afar off eyes,
> Though it contain no place for me.
> (Hardy 1978: 94)

What if there is no place for us in heaven? Or, to put it another way: what if, by excluding all sorts of people from it (roughly classed as heretics and sinners) we deprive ourselves of the kind of joy associated with heaven? There is, after all, a warning about this from Jesus. He is reported to have said that 'there is more joy in heaven over one sinner who repents [presumably on earth] than over those who are "righteous"' (Luke 15:7). In case we still have not got his message another gospel writer repeats it: 'Amen, amen I say to you: Harlots and sinners will go first into the kingdom of heaven!' (Matthew 21:31).

That's not all we can read out of Hardy's conjecture. He provides another revolutionary twist to our perception of ourselves and of heaven when he wonders if there's any place at all for us in what we call Paradise. Are we, he muses, the excluded rather than the excluders? If we are prepared to say, on God's behalf, that we are the *only* creature on earth God willed for itself then theologically it makes sense to think that the same God wills us to be the *only* creature in heaven. But, Hardy says, suppose it is the other way around? Suppose Paradise is inhabited by all other species, but not by us? Is it for those 'bare lifers' with just a voice, but not for us with our language skills? Is it inhabited, perhaps, by those who have no voice? By those plant forms whose ceaseless, silent and creative labour ensures that the sun's energy is processed for others, especially us. And finally, does it include what we most want excluded: death?

For what is Paradise without trees? Scientist Tyler Volk advises us to run our hands along the thick, corrugated bark of a tree and feel its deeply fissured epidermis. Inside it lie some vital layers of cells, some dead, some alive. First comes a shallow layer called the phloem. Its vertical columns of cells are alive but are on their way to a planned death. Next comes a thin generative layer that contains the actual living cells of the trunk. These cells reproduce to create all the other layers, both outward and inward. Inside the generative layer is the zone called the xylem. It has columns of tubes and its cells are dead.

The xylem's function, notes Volk, is to move the mineral-laden water gathered by the roots up to the needles or leaves. Its dead cells are called tracheids. When grouped into units they not only provide water and mineral circulation but also support against gravity. Without tracheids, he says, there would be no green life on land except some ground-hugging tiny mosses and soil crust with green bacteria and algae. For not only trees contain tracheids, but so do all non-woody plants in their stems, branches, stalks and in the veins of leaves: '*These dead parts remain as functional units within the tree or small plant, absolutely vital to its life*' (Volk 2002: 181–183. My italics).

So if there is a tree in Paradise and it yields fruit (as we are told in Revelation 22:2) this can only happen if dead tracheids keep the mineral-laden water flowing to feed the leaves and the blossom. And when the blossom dies, if an insect or bird has pollinated it the seeds of future life drop to the ground because the cells holding them to the stem have died. We find that if Paradise is as we imagine it, we cannot exclude death from it either.

There are 'immortal' organisms, ones that can be killed but do not naturally die, such as bacteria or amoebae. But the evolution of multicellular beings like ourselves included death, and it was the invention of death that made possible the existence of our brains. And it is one of the central ironies of human existence, says biologist Ursula Goodenough, that it is our sentient brains that are capable of experiencing sorrow and fear at the prospect of our own death, and of dreaming of a life beyond it (Goodenough 1998: 143–150).

Our health, our wholeness and our capacity for joy is sustained every moment on earth by interactions between life and death, both in our own bodies and in those of others. The type of interaction with death is unique to each moment and to each living being whose life cannot continue without it. We deceive ourselves then if we imagine our lives continuing forever in a death-free zone we call 'heaven'. Hardy's poem expands the framework in which we think about life, before death as well as after it, by shaking our (now largely unstated) belief in being chosen to live forever – without death. And so he shifts not only our perspective on heaven, but also on ourselves and on our lives on earth.

7   Life on earth

Hardy is not the only poet whose vision shifted my perspective on heaven. Another one, e.e. cummings, does so by juxtaposing the two following images and implicitly asking us to choose which we ourselves prefer:

> I'd rather learn from one bird how to sing
> than teach ten thousand stars how not to dance.
> (cummings 1960: 40)

As decisively as Hardy, these two lines reverse the usual trend of human aspiration. Which of us would learn from a bird rather than teach ten thousand stars? No matter that we do not have the choice. What matters is by deciding, we show whether or not we take seriously our membership of an earthly rather than a heavenly community. Are we content to belong to it and to learn from others within it who count for little in terms of the power they wield? Or do we see ourselves as teachers of the universe, epistemologically privileged enough to control the stars? cummings asks us to look at what makes life within the earth community a wonderful, life-long learning experience – rather than setting our sights on an unattainable, self-aggrandizing life located in 'the heavens'. The image of one fragile, mortal bird, set against that of numerous mighty and seemingly everlasting stars, questions our image of ourselves and of our true place and role on earth. Do we accept that place, or, on the evidence of the previous chapter, except ourselves from it?

This echo from the previous chapter – of the notion of human exceptionalism in regard to life and death on earth – takes us straight into the subject of this chapter: the role of death in life. The image of the singing bird has, of course, many symbolic overtones in relation to death. John Keats was stressing his own mortality when he wrote in his 'Ode to a Nightingale': '*Thou* wast not born for death, immortal Bird!' However the image of a bird can carry the opposite and here more pertinent connotation too.

Pictures of Jesus as a child in Mary's arms, seated under or near a barren tree, often include a bird (usually a black crow) perched on a bare branch. This, we are told, is a symbol of death. Its primary purpose is to symbolize Jesus's impending death. But its perch, the barren tree, is also intended as a reminder of its opposite: the immortal tree in Paradise whose leaves do not fade or fall.

For death plays no part in the traditional image of heaven. Heaven is defined as the opposite of earth precisely by excluding from it anything or anyone touched by death or its religious proxies: corruption, decadence and sin. Heavenly life excludes all living things on earth that rely on death to sustain them: the dead tracheid cells, for example, in the stems and branches of plant forms ranging from grass to tree. A traditional heaven would (logically) exclude all trees that yield fruit and all mortal birds from whom we might learn to sing.

Such a limited (and limiting) vision tells us far more about ourselves than it does about heaven. It tells us that naturally we find the thought of dying (and the pain and sorrow that usually surround it) so terrifying that we exclude it from life as much as possible. Therefore we would, if we could, banish it altogether from our existence. And so our 'heaven' is a place where no one dies.

But this, as we saw in the previous chapter, is the most clear example of our desire to exclude ourselves from the evolutionary community of life on earth. For the fact is that death powers the evolution of life. Dying is an integral part of being alive – for us as for all living beings. 'The secrets of evolution,' Carl Sagan wrote in 1985, 'are death and time – the deaths of enormous numbers of life forms and the time required for a long succession of small mutations that were by accident adaptive.' In 1994 he was faced with this reality himself when, diagnosed as having a rare blood disease, he had to work out his response to the evolutionary presence of death in his own life. Shortly before he died (in 1996) he wrote that while he would like to believe in an afterlife, the world is so exquisite that it seems far better 'to look Death in the eye and be grateful every day for the brief but magnificent opportunity life provides' (Sagan 1997: 257, 266).

His gratitude for this opportunity is based on his acceptance of death as inescapable if life on earth is to continue. In the light of that understanding he affirms the wonder and joy of being alive. His exemplary response reveals an understanding of what it means to be a member of the whole community of life on earth: one continuously supported and sustained by the death of countless of its members, from the smallest and apparently least significant bacterium to the mightiest tree.

Therefore it is hardly surprising that the western tradition of human exceptionalism manifests itself most decisively in our desire to except our-

selves from the evolutionary history of life on earth: one that progresses
through death. Whether or not this exception is made on religious grounds,
by making it we implicitly except ourselves not only from the community
of earthly life but from the life of earth itself. For we know now that
the earth too is mortal: destined to die, perhaps, when the sun finally
implodes. The claim to exemption from death, from mortality, is therefore
the most extreme form of the claim to a purely homocentric universe:
one made solely 'for us' – in which we live forever. And since this is not
possible on earth, we imagine immortal life enjoyed in heaven to be our
true destiny.

Yet the fear of death that drives us to make this ultimate claim is itself
evidence of a fundamental biological bond between us and all sentient
beings. All respond spontaneously to the threat of death, usually through
fight or flight but also with what can appear to us as acceptance or resigna-
tion. (The role played by us in inflicting violent death on others in increasingly horrific ways throughout human history has, of course, increased our
terror in the face of it. But I am talking here about the natural process of
dying.) Other more considered, less immediate responses are also open to
us that, as Sagan's dying shows, help us react to death's approach in a more
grateful, generous and gentle spirit.

Tyler Volk developed such a conscious response when, poisoned by
carbon monoxide, he had to face the realization that someday he really
would die. And perhaps quite soon. He fought against the fear and horror
generated by this with the joyous recognition of how happy he was to have
been alive. He consciously decided that he would continue to be thankful
for this if granted another day. So, like Sagan, he proposes that 'we greet
not Death, but Life with simple gratitude'. Gratitude for life is, he says, the
self-conscious response for dealing with the fears engendered by death
(Volk 2002: 65–67).

Death and life in a heliocentric community

There are powerful echoes here of Hardy's and Sagan's responses to the
possibility of being excluded from Paradise. There are communal responses
to death too that on closer inspection reveal some features related to these
individual ones. Funeral rituals generally, as a consciously considered
response to death, necessarily invoke a vision of that larger order in which
the social life of the group is linked to 'all that dies and all that cannot die'
(Dante). At that time life becomes that bit more transcendent for each individual. Death's visible presence awakens the consciousness of the living not
only to the tie that is broken but also to the ties that are maintained
between each of us and the dead. Life and death together are seen not only

as aspects of the larger body of human society but of the larger body still of the whole community of life on earth.

I grew up in Ireland within easy distance of the Boyne Valley Neolithic passage tombs at a time when they were rarely visited. So I was able to enter the one at Newgrange. A slender opening between massive stones leads to a long narrow passage ending at the central burial chamber. The stones there are so angled that on mid-winter's day the light of the sun penetrates into the very centre of the tomb: 'showing the living and the dead that, as in nature's annual cycle, there is a new beginning after the darkness of death is passed' (Brennan 1990: 145; see also O'Kelly 1982). Human self-consciousness here transcends its own bounds within a truly sun-centred world.

The acknowledgement of and reverence for sun-centredness in preliterate cultures survived in Europe (where many such tombs have been found) at a subliminal level. It supported the later scientific, philosophical and religiously symbolic heliocentrism that flourished again at the time of Copernicus. The annual 'return' of the sun in winter as it journeys around the earth has always given an unpredictable edge to life that arouses wonder, curiosity and awe: even now when we can calculate and presumably count on its return for some billions of years. In pre-urban cultures in the Northern hemisphere the visible penetration of earth's winter darkness by a brilliant shaft of sunlight was a guarantee that life would continue and death would not prevail. At the same time it was a physical reminder of our absolute dependence on the annual earthly growth cycle that was itself dependent on the sun's renewed and freely given energy.

This natural framework for human existence was and is one in which darkness and light necessarily alternate, define and enhance each other and visibly move our lives on from past to present to future. As a solar myth it gave preliterate societies a conceptual framework within which metaphors of light and darkness could and still do express complex relationships between life and death. The tombs speak eloquently, in terms of light and darkness, of the human experience of the generation, death and regeneration of life. The darkening of the sun, source of light and life, was experienced as if *it* were dying. By siting their ancestral graves at the exact point of the sun's 'rebirth' at winter solstice, those who built them not only expressed their trust in its renewing life but also alluded to the fact that they, their ancestors and the planet were, to use Wallace Stevens's phrase, 'makings of the sun'. So the dead buried in darkness and the seeds buried in earth would both, in due course, be revivified in some fashion by the sun's light.

Pre-Christian burials of this type (under a huge mound of earth raised over a massive stone structure) testify to sophisticated notions of the afterlife in preliterate cultures. The architecture, both actually and symbolically, represents our common human journey: from life to death to new life; from light to darkness to new light; to 'a new beginning after the darkness of death has passed'. Within deep time as now understood it can also represent the journey of our species, like all others, from its hidden beginnings in earthly, material substances to life in the sun's light followed eventually by our return to earth. And ultimately, perhaps, to our definitive oneness with earth in the sun's final implosion.[12]

Darkness and light

The experiential and symbolic coincidence of darkness and light in the cre-ation and re-creation of life is a recurring motif in religious accounts of the creation of the world. The opening lines of the biblical version in Genesis, Steven Rose remarks, is no exception. They are so familiar that in a sense none of us reads the story for the first time, central as it is to Jewish, Chris-tian and Islamic traditions. Perhaps surprisingly, he says, on re-reading it as an ex-orthodox Jew, an atheist and a biologist to boot, he finds that its claims as to who we humans are, and our complex relationships to nature – including our own, human nature – underlie many of the presuppositions of our assumedly post-religious, rationalist and reductionist modern science, however forcefully we dismiss the biblical version (Rose 1998: viii). The role played by the figure of 'Adam' is, as we have seen, a case in point.

To reduce the familiarity slightly (Rose was introducing a new edition of the well-known King James version) I shall use Mary Phil Korsak's literal (word for word) translation of the Hebrew original that runs as follows:

> At the start Elohim created the skies and the earth
> – the earth was tohu-bohu [untranslatable]
> darkness on the face of the deep
> and the breath of Elohim
> hovering on the face of the waters –
> Elohim said
> Let light be
> Light was
> Elohim saw the light. 'How good!'
> Elohim separated the light from the darkness
> Elohim called to the light 'Day'
> To the darkness he called 'Night'.
> (Korsak 1993: 1)

Countless religious reflections on this text over the years have consistently emphasised the 'goodness' of light and, by covert comparison or implication, the lack of goodness in darkness. This has so shaped cultural notions of good and bad that the cognates of darkness (death, shadows, night, sunless depths) have come to symbolize all that is considered bad or evil. No one thought Ann Widdecombe was paying a compliment to her fellow politician, Michael Howard, when she said: 'He has something of the night in him'! The identification of evil with darkness of skin is poignantly described by James Baldwin in his account of French children running away from him in terror because they had never seen a black man before and thought he was the devil (Baldwin 1990). Reaction to and recognition of this deep-rooted and so almost instinctive prejudice has, thankfully, led to a notable resistance to this particular form of it. However there is still a long way to go in becoming aware of such connotations: not least in religious discourse.

I found this to be the case at a religious conference entitled *Moving toward a new dawn!* The title was depicted in symbols characterizing a movement from black to white, from night to day, with an accompanying exhortation to leave 'darkness' behind and move 'toward the light of Christ'. One of my fellow speakers, an African Asian, began his address with a courteous but incisive reminder to his audience of the impossibility, not to mention the undesirability, of his leaving his colour behind in order to draw nearer to Christ.

The colouring of vice and virtue by their identification with black and white, light and darkness, good and evil, night and day, death and life is a subject with vast cultural and political implications. My interest here is the role this identification plays in religious discourse and in particular, in the presupposition that God lives in, indeed *is* 'the Light of life'. To use the symbol of the sun or of its light to speak about God is perfectly legitimate. It becomes problematic when its use is taken to exclude any possibility that God also inhabits darkness or is at home with death.

But that is precisely what the Genesis text says. In fact, the primary presence of God (Elohim) is of the divine breath hovering (with an intimation of loving attention) over the dark waters. Indeed, if we so wish, the ambiguity of the Hebrew allows us to identify 'the breath of Elohim' *with* 'the darkness on the face of the deep'. This biblical tradition is clearly evident in the Psalms where we are told quite plainly that darkness, death and light are all alike to God. 'If I walk through the dark valley of death I fear no evil for you, O God, are with me there' (Psalm 23:4).

My point here is that to link death with darkness and life with light has meant, religiously, assuming that death is 'not-God': either in the sense of being part of God's original intention for us and so an intrinsic part of human life, or of being 'good'. So our natural, biological and inchoate fear of dying/death/darkness, clearly evident in funerals and other rituals, has been given a particularly cutting edge by its religious association with death as something that could separate us from God: as divine punishment for sin.

This destroys the natural, essential connection between darkness and light, death and life and finally, between earth and 'heaven' as God's dwelling place. For if earth is mortal too then it cannot, so the theo-logic runs, be the dwelling place of an 'immortal' God. But, says Genesis, God's breath 'hovers over' the darkness of earth's deeps. And God separated light from darkness in order to name light 'Day' and darkness 'Night': not in order to condemn one or the other but in order to establish the diurnal rhythm of creation. Natural growth requires darkness and rest as much as light and activity. Unless the seed is buried deep in the darkness of earth it remains alone. And, says the psalmist, God accompanies us through both death and life to the very end – and to whatever we imagine lies beyond.

A glance at another religious tradition may help clarify my point without, I hope, doing that tradition an injustice by simplifying a very complex set of concepts. In her discussion of 'root metaphors' in Taoism (a classification that with its organic overtones says much about how they emerge and evolve) Sarah Allan says that the complementary forces that imbue and define all life came be known as *yin*, darkness, and *yang*, light. Both terms were originally associated with landscape. *Yin* refers to the shaded areas of a river valley and the term is conventionally used to describe dark valleys and rain. *Yang*, on the other hand, refers to bright mountain peaks. She makes the point that this complementary pair came to subsume other earlier ones, including water and fire, female and male, below and above. And that *Yin* and *Yang*, as principles that refer to the physical world (darkness and light, valleys and mountains, water and fire) are also applied to human life and society (Allan 1997: 58–61).

Allan's point that darkness and light symbolize the complementary forces and principles that imbue and define all life is important here. As is the fact that they have an undisputed reference to the physical world even when used as abstract concepts. Her defining them as 'root metaphors' is itself a metaphor for the organic growth of language forms based on analogy with the physical world. It is hardly surprising then that the common human experience of that world is also expressed in the Hebrew account of the origins of life on earth as water/darkness and sun-fire/light.

It is not surprising either that when I asked James Lovelock to clarify some point about Gaia's evolution he wrote on the customary back of an envelope as follows:

In the beginning
the Earth evolved chemically and physically.
Sometime after its birth
the first living organisms appeared,
probably at a single place.
Gradually
life spread over most of the planet.
It was mostly ocean.
During this period life and Earth evolved separately.
As life grew abundant
it began to change the environment
until its evolution and the Earth's evolution
merged into a single process:
the dynamic system
Gaia

(Personal communication, April 1999)

The important thing about his account is that, as in the Genesis text, the potential for the creation of life lies in 'the waters' of earth. Scientists generally agree that it was from this 'deep time' ocean, then covering most of the earth, that living entities did in fact emerge. Their emergence was made possible because the life-giving properties characterizing the water of those oceans had themselves evolved through change and interaction powered by some form of death.

Watching the water in a creek flow over his hand, Tyler Volk asks: where was its source? Geographically, in the mountains miles upstream. Prior to that, in the snowfall that was melting in the mountains. What about the creation of the atoms that compose the snow water? Its hydrogen was made about thirteen billion years ago. Water's other component, oxygen, was forged in a series of fusions that took hydrogen into heavier elements. Here, he says, is a case in the realm of physics of 'death, thus life'. For in a sense, the hydrogen dies to form oxygen. This life from death is life of another entity, oxygen in this case, which later combines with some of that abundant, still living, primordial hydrogen, 'giving birth to water that now nourishes the algae and my life. In looking at how death becomes life we invariably have to shift scales in types of entities, often upward to the larger encompassing context' (Volk 2002: 224f.).

Speaking of death

Recalling Sarah Allan's point about the association between landscape and root metaphors, I want to draw attention to the difficulty, for non-scientists like myself, of holding fast to that association when abstract scientific terms and symbols, like those of mathematics or the atomic structure of elements, are used to shift scales up or down. This symbolic shift necessarily involves detaching or distancing the water before me into symbols that detach the water from any landscape. That distancing also occurs, of course, in the routine use of tapwater. And I am aware that common use of the word 'water' and scientific use of the term 'H_2O' does not make either usage identical with the being of water. In the latter case, however, the symbols, as abstract mental constructs, can distance me even further from the reality of water flowing over my hand, even though understanding its structure at the atomic scale can and does give a dimension to my knowledge of it that no amount of direct experience could convey. How else could I learn that I would not now exist without the death of some hydrogen molecules in the deep time of earth's evolution?

Nevertheless there are dangers in abstraction, among them the very real and present danger of our being so distanced from any landscape that we no longer realize how deeply we are rooted in it and it in us. I alluded to this before when remarking on the way in which urbanization has led to our apparently living in a humanly created environment. Hence the concept of the 'ecological footprint' was developed to remind us that, in fact, each of us makes an identifiable imprint on earth's resources (albeit one invisible to us) because we depend on and consume quantifiable amounts of them. And to remind us that we also deplete them directly in various ways, notably in our collective generation of waste and in our personal need to excrete bodily waste.

Covering earth with pavements and buildings is a fairly obvious way of distancing ourselves from it and all it means for us. There is, however, a rather less obvious but no less powerful form of distancing from the physical landscape that permeates our culture. This is the process of commodifying it: of turning all our relations with it into commodity exchanges (Primavesi 2000: 101–105).

My most recent visit to Newgrange brought this home to me in no uncertain terms, for the Boyne Valley site has become a blatant example of this process of commodification. My first visit there, many years ago, was a whole-body, unquantifiable experience, one whose impact has, if anything, increased with time – particularly as I learn more about the people who made it, why they did so, and what that, and they, mean to me today. There was no question then of *detaching* the site (or myself) from the land-scape in abstract terms by commodifying it as a 'thing' one paid to see.

Now, however, Newgrange exhibits this abstraction and detachment in every sense and at every level of experience. It and the larger neighbouring tombs of Dowth and Knowth have been painstakingly excavated, their contents analysed, dated, quantified and labelled and the whole enclosed within an area of highly restricted access. A tastefully designed visitors centre has been constructed at a distance in which, after paying an entrance fee, one can look at an exhibition simulating prehistoric life and the building of the tombs and study the analyses of the materials and building methods. There is a video reconstruction of a winter solstice and for a further fee, a short guided trip by bus to one or other tomb. But a fibreglass reconstruction of one such tomb at the visitors' centre conveys the message to visitors that they need not visit a real tomb if short of time and energy.

The intrinsic value of Newgrange is almost completely lost in this commodification process. The results rouse no more than curiosity or doubt as to their accuracy or, more positively, some appreciation of the ingenuity and technical ability shown in the construction of some of the artefacts. But they could not arouse any sense of wonder in me at the mystery of life and death in a heliocentric world. Nor did they arouse gratitude for my being alive to see them at this particular moment in my species' journey from deep time. I was distracted from what they stand for. For they had been wholly detached from the landscape and become a simulacrum of Neolithic, heliocentric life.

My distancing from the tombs involved a series of commodity exchanges: between landscape and artefact; between stone and video screen; between birdsong and recording; between me and the money I paid to see the commodities. Together they provided a virtual reality instead of the real one. Indeed, for some visitors, the distancing and substitution are inescapable. For the visitor numbers are so great that at peak times it is necessary to book a day ahead for the bus trip to an actual tomb. Those who go unaware of this, as I did, must settle for the virtual reality. The real tomb remains a vague shape in the distance.

There are perfectly valid reasons for excluding me and others from the actual site, not least the escalating numbers of visitors. But the distance between us and the physical landscape of Newgrange epitomizes how distanced most of us are now from physical, direct exchanges with earth's landscape and with the individual and communal realities of death and life that sustain it. We are not only distant in space and time from the deep time creation of the landscape itself, and from the people who billions of years later lived and died there and built the tombs. We are increasingly distanced from our earthiness, and from the reality of death. Our attention is focused instead on commodity exchanges: between ourselves and between us and the landscape. So that we ourselves, like the visitors to Newgrange, are increasingly treated as units of commercial value.

An extreme example will make my point. In 1998 I read an account of a British county council that refused to pay for the funeral of a poor resident who had died in a private home, on the grounds that 'from a commercial point of view, residents of a home are its income-producing raw material. Therefore, from a purely commercial point of view, deceased residents may be regarded as the waste products of the business' (*Guardian* 7 August 1998).

This is a stark reminder of the momentum towards a product-based valuation of everything, including ourselves, inherent in commodification: one increased through our ability to manipulate computer data in which 'plus' or 'minus' commercial value is routinely assigned to products. In many and various ways our commercial value is abstracted and used to assess our worth. And as this happens, it becomes more and more difficult to see life on earth in Sagan's terms: as a brief but magnificent opportunity; as a gift to which gratitude and wonder are appropriate responses.

In the final chapters of *Sacred Gaia* I used the notion of 'gift event' to describe this alternative type of exchange between us and earth and within the earth community. It is one in which no symbol of commodity value is attached to what is given that would then allow us to detach the symbol from it and use that as a token substitute for the exchange between us and the giver. How could I pay a bird to teach me how to sing? What cash token corresponds to its freely given song?

The primary, unquantifiable gift considered in this chapter, that of life, is one whose true value and sacredness becomes increasingly apparent as we learn, often painfully, that it cannot be captured in a net of words or concepts, in a handful of coins or in an immortal body. Nor can it exist separated from its dependence on death. In the summer of 1225 Francis of Assisi responded to death's approach in exemplary fashion when, in constant pain and almost blind, he composed the poem popularly known as 'The Canticle of the Sun'. It begins with praise of God the most high. It then goes on to praise God 'through all that God has made'. 'And first my lord Brother Sun who brings the day; and light you give us through him. How beautiful is he, how radiant in all his splendour!' Naming other powers and elements as members of his earth family, Francis notes what each one gives us in life: Sister Moon and Stars, Brothers Wind and Air, Sister Water, Brother Fire and 'Sister Earth, our Mother'. Some few days before his death he composed the final verses in which he praises God through 'Sister Death, from whose embrace no mortal can escape'.

This poet, legend tells us, may indeed have learned his song from the birds. As death approached, Francis saw it too as a gift of God; as one whose embrace holds all (mortal) life together. His joyful awareness of the gift of life saw it inextricably intertwined with the gift of death: both gifts given and responded to in continuous exchanges between him and other members of the whole earth community.

8   Gift exchanges

What awareness is there today of life, never mind death, as a gift? One to be met with gratitude and used to increase our joyful awareness of what it means to be alive? A particular response from Glynn Gorick to the notion of gift event/exchange developed in the final chapters of *Sacred Gaia* helps answer these questions. (He is the artist who painted the cover picture for that book and for this one.)

He read those chapters at a time when he was illustrating the UNESCO introductory booklet for the *Encyclopaedia of Life Support Systems* (EOLSS) published at the time of the World Summit on Sustainable Development in Johannesburg in 2002. His task was to show the differences between the human system of economic accounting and the natural flows of energy and materials within the associated cycles and systems that constitute the planetary biosphere system. The basic idea behind both types is that the systems work through exchanges. In natural systems energy builds in positive feedback and stabilizes in negative feedback. In the business world this is understood as inputs/outputs accumulation.

After reading the final chapters of *Sacred Gaia*, Gorick wrote:

> The startling point in *Sacred Gaia* which may expand this view is the process of giving. This in its true sense seems to be outside of a systems view, as energy is given without any design for feedback. As you say, it is not logical, not scientific or physics; maybe it is in the realm of metaphysics. I have a feeling that this is a quality item of very high power that is not measurable and plays a huge role in the evolution and stability/security of communities. It may be the mystery factor 'altruism' which puzzles evolutionary biologists. I have a hunch that it features in the background sense of distress which fortunate communities have while dealing with the process of living with business as usual while vast numbers of impoverished people subsist and perish within and without a global system. The process of

giving in its purest and most powerful sense makes standard economic nonsense.

How is it that it survives in cultures as a tangible characteristic of being human when it seems to be contrary to the laws of conservation of energy or the logic of genes being selected for advantage over other genes? There seems to be a connection here with our understanding of what love means and perhaps its central position in the tricky area of ethics and morality (and spirituality)...

(Personal communication)

Such responses as this to my discussion of gift made me realize the enduring and contemporary importance of the *practice* of gift exchange, even though such practice is generally seen to belong within the context of pre-industrial cultures. Yet the *theory* of 'gift' (derived in large part from the anthropological studies of Mauss and others) is now the subject of vigorous philosophical, cultural and theological debate.

In this chapter I want to bring the practice and the theory of gift exchange together. The main point I want to take from the theoretical debate is one agreed on by Derrida and Marion (they disagree about most other aspects of the gift concept): 'We cannot explain, and we have no access to the gift, so long as we keep it within the horizon of economy' (Caputo 1999: 56–62).

Gorick makes the same point (rather more forthrightly) when he says that the process of giving, in its purest and most powerful sense, makes standard economic nonsense. But this also makes it, as he points out, a necessary counterweight to the now generally accepted view that the constant and essential energy exchanges between us and between us and other members of the earth community can be systematized and expressed in abstract terms of feedback (whether positive or negative; whether credit or debit; whether material, monetary or otherwise).

By contrast, the essential character of gift exchange is a refusal to consider those exchanges solely, if at all, in those terms. Whatever is given is given away *freely*: that is, it is not expected to return to the giver with its commercial value or its usefulness increased. Indeed, it is not expected to bring return to the giver in any perceivable form. However there is sometimes a recognition of the giver by the recipient, or at least the desire to express gratitude to the provider of the gift. Whereas within the free market system, as we shall see, there is practically no possibility of the provider being thanked or of the source of the commodity being recognized.

This last use of the term 'free' bears no relation to the freedom exercised by the giver within gift exchange. That has practically disappeared in the current market economy where the 'freedom' of the market signifies the free use by strong economies of their market dominance. In other words, it stands for their being free to increase their share of profits from the commodification of natural resources. The word 'free' in gift exchange signifies an exchange in which there is no expectation of gain, capital or otherwise. These very different concepts of freedom in relation to the expected outcome of exchange underline the stark contrast between the practice of gift exchange and the systematized economic and scientific models of energy exchange that are the norm today. They are designed to yield something quantifiably in excess of what is given.

In the preceding chapter I described this most commonly experienced and normative type of exchange as commodity exchange. Its hidden effect is to make relations between people appear as relations between things (Primavesi 2000: 101f.). It also, of course (as we saw in the case of Newgrange), affects relations between people and their environments. It does this by distancing those who use money in exchange for commodities from those who earn money by making those commodities; and distances both groups (to whom we all belong) from the natural resources used in making the commodities. These natural resources (described in EOLSS as 'natural capital'), extracted from the earth in ever-increasing amounts, are abstracted into units of raw material processed into commodities. The commodities are then quantified in various ways and sold as products with a given cash value.

Each step in the abstraction process distances us further from the one who provides the actual commodity and from its material base in natural life-support systems. The distancing process is complete when the commodity is abstracted into cash units and the cash we exchange for those units is itself exchanged for cash. This distances us mentally as well as physically from the all-encompassing life-support system of the global environment to such an extent that we can and do all too easily lose any awareness of it. And of the fact that

> [H]umanity is just a small part of a huge inter-dependent self-regulating system. The global environment recycles gases, water and wastes, and is the source of food, timber, minerals and energy. Humanity has blandly accepted the belief that global cycles and circulation systems will maintain the supply of vital components and, as a result of this belief, often has had little regard for how these systems can be strained beyond the point of natural recovery.
>
> (EOLSS 2002: 28)

Even less regard is paid to the fact that the huge, interdependent, self-regulating global environment is a gift to all earth's inhabitants: it gives the necessities of life to all members of the earth community: human and non-human. So if the gift aspect of our relationship with earth is ignored and the sources of what we receive go unrecognized, responses to the supply of vital components we receive are reduced to our saying (as Rilke notes): 'It's mine!' We take those components and turn them into possessions; into commodities to be traded for other possessions. Above all, we trade those commodities for cash profit. When this happens on a global scale, as it now does, we are in effect treating the earth as a possession to be traded for monetary advantage. This premise, and its conclusion, was expressed succinctly by an anonymous nineteenth-century Native American:

> Only when the last tree has died and the last river has been poisoned and the last fish has been caught will we realize that we cannot eat money.

Those of our own species who run out of cash, not to mention all other species who do not deal in this currency, already find themselves left without anything to exchange for the vital components essential to sustain their lives. And then they may, and tragically do, starve to death.

The nature of gift exchange

These are some of the visible effects of the loss of a gift exchange culture, summed up in human terms by the rising poverty levels in an increasingly commodified and 'developed' economy. Given that fact, it seems more important than ever to point to an alternative form of exchange between us and our global environment. But enough has been said to show that gift exchange, as generally practised and understood, is not an obvious or easy option. Not only does it presuppose a sense of belonging to a group or place as well as a sense of dependence on common resources. Its proper practice ultimately requires seeing the vital components of one's life as gifts from other living beings: gifts often given to us through their death. And as they have been freely given, they have to be received and treated as gifts: not as possessions.

This fact confronts us most plainly at every meal, where life and death are inextricably intertwined in 'the planet on the table'. If we recognize this phenomenon for what it is, we may say, with Dolores La Chapelle:

> We give-away our thanks to the sun
> Who gives-away warmth and light.
> All beings on earth: the trees, the animals, the wind
> And the rivers give-away to one another
> So all is in balance.
>
> (Roberts 1991: 239)

The dominance of commodity exchange, however, at best dulls and at worst destroys our sense of gratitude or any desire to 'give-away' in our turn. In societies characterized by mobility and distanced from the landscape through technological and urbanized environments, priority is given to economic exchanges rather than to the common or global life systems that support them. The vital components taken from them are processed and used in ways that guarantee a cash return. Members of these societies are counted (literally) as suppliers or consumers of goods and services (such as health, education, security, entertainment and mobility). The goods and services are systematized in different ways (in terms of input and output flows) and paid for through increasingly impersonalized monetary transactions. Electronic information exchange about quantity, components, price and performance determines the course of these transactions. As does our ability to meet the price. In societies where the physical, public infrastructures are seen solely as a source of income, either through taxes, grants or shares, these infrastructures are distorted from their common purpose of providing vital benefits, such as clean water, to all citizens (Primavesi 2000: 111–112). This problem was the subject of much discussion at Johannesburg and led to a commitment to finding some solution to it.

The contrast between this situation and that found in a gift exchange culture emerges clearly in Lewis Hyde's description of life among the Native American tribes that occupied the Pacific coast of North America before it was opened to white traders by Captain Cook in the late eighteenth century. All the tribes depended on the ocean to provide their primary sustenance. Above all they depended on the salmon that entered the coastal rivers annually and swam upriver to spawn. They believed that all animals lived as they did – in tribes – and that the salmon tribe dwelt in a huge lodge beneath the sea. According to this mythology, there they have human form but, once a year, they change into fish bodies dressed in robes of salmon skin, swim to the mouth of the rivers and voluntarily sacrifice themselves so that their land brothers may have food for the winter.

The tribes expressed this understanding of the relationship between them and the salmon by ritualizing it in a cycle of gifts. The first salmon to appear in the rivers was given an elaborate welcome. A priest or his assistant would catch it, parade it to an altar and lay it out before the group. Its body was sprinkled with eagle down or red ochre and a formal speech of welcome was made. Everyone sang the songs that welcome an honoured guest. After the ceremony the priest gave everyone present a piece of the fish.

> Finally – and this is what makes it clearly a gift cycle – the bones of the
> first salmon were returned to the sea. The belief was that salmon bones
> placed back into the water would reassemble once they had washed out

to sea; the fish would then revive, return to its home, and revert to human form. The skeleton of the first salmon had to be returned to the water intact; later fish could be cut apart, but all their bones were still put back into the water. If not, the salmon would be offended and might not return the following years with their gift of winter food.

(Hyde 1999: 26f.)

Hyde comments that, as in other first-fruits rituals such as those of the Maori or the Jews, the lesson of the myth is that the objects of the ritual will remain plentiful *because* they are treated as gifts. The ceremony establishes a gift relationship with nature: a formal give-and-take that acknowledges our participation in, and our dependence upon natural increase.

And where we have established such a relationship we tend to respond to nature as a part of ourselves, not as a stranger or an alien available for exploitation. Gift exchange brings with it, therefore, a built-in check upon the destruction of its objects; with it we will not destroy nature's renewable wealth except where we also consciously destroy ourselves.

(Hyde 1999: 26f.)

The subtleties of gift exchange, says Hyde, always become more apparent when set alongside commodity exchange. He proves his point by describing what happened when the Hudson's Bay Company established its first outposts on the North Pacific coast in the 1830s. The company wanted to trade furs, and did not molest the Indians. However the company's presence affected them nonetheless, for with it came firearms, sails and alcohol. The Indians began to winter near the company stores, depending more and more on a market they did not control. Towards the end of the century whites began to commercialize the salmon fishing. The Indians were not recognized as full citizens and could not file land claims whereas a white entrepreneur could simply stake off 80 acres on each side of a river mouth, build a cannery and shop and, when he had more salmon than he needed, might or might not allow the Indians to fish. They had then to buy foodstuffs and to buy them they needed cash. To acquire cash they had to work in the salmon factory where they were paid by the day. So they had to buy food on credit, work to pay off their debts and return next season to continue the cycle of work, food, credit and debt (Hyde 1999: 29f.).[13]

The present context for gift exchange

This clear and poignant example of the shift from a gift exchange culture (that responds to its life-support systems with ritual expressions of gratitude and sharing of the gifts) to one based solely on commodity exchange invites many different kinds of response. One is to dismiss the whole notion. For Hyde's context may seem so remote that it bears little relation to ours, not least in its mythic vision of the connections between the salmon's life and that of the tribe and in its perception of our own lives being destroyed when we destroy the life of other species.

But a moment's reflection on the four opening chapters of this book reminds us that equally mythic visions influence contemporary western culture in all kinds of ways: Plato's *Timaeus* as revisioned by Christians comes to mind. True, these revisions focus on 'the heavens' rather than 'the waters of the sea'. But that surely made them *more* mythical, in the generally accepted sense of being a solely imaginative exercise without the empirical evidence of the salmon's annual return. Yet they remain powerful enough, as we know, to govern much of western cultural and religious imagination. Above all, they continue to influence our perception of how we are related to earth: as 'controlling' minds rather than dependent bodies.

My concern here is neither with the concept of myth nor with the controversy surrounding the term when it is used to dismiss the truth claims of religious views in terms of a necessary progress from 'mythos' to 'logos', that is, as if myth is always opposed to, or incompatible with, rationality. As Gwen Griffith-Dickson points out, setting myth and rationality against one another in this way makes myth, at best, carry the blame for the failures of rationality. With her (and by inference, with Gorick), I would suggest that in the contemporary context of the 'myth' of the 'free' market, we need to be aware of other, opposing forms of myth in order to assess the truth and justice of the 'market's' rationality (Griffith-Dickson 2000: 64–66).

For myth has a necessary, continuing, and now largely unacknowledged function within societies. Briefly, myth offers a focus for thought; puts people in touch not only with the minds of their contemporaries but with those of their forebears and ancestors; validates present practice in terms of a wider picture both in time and space; and provides a net of ideas and attitudes that guarantee one's identity within a group (McLeish 1996: v). And as Hyde pointed out, myth is a way of teaching us the kind of relationships with nature that support rather than destroy a community's life.

Within that understanding of myth and its function, we can now see a myth – even more ancient than any of Plato's – functioning again within western culture: the myth of Gaia, the self-regulating 'Self' of a female earth deity. In Hesiod's *Theogony*, Gaia, or earth, is the primordial cosmic goddess who is also a primal earth deity. The first children of Gaia are features of nature: Heaven, Hills and Sea. Her marriages with her children lead to the emergence of generations of gods through vertical genealogies: union with the Heavens creates one going through the Titans to Zeus. By

Hesiod's time Zeus's descendants/gods most closely resembled those historic humans who, like him, imposed their will and rule on others during Greek prehistory (Nelson 1998: 44–47).

This genealogical narrative is not, of course, the way in which the myth is now being told. Instead of a narrative poem describing the gradual emergence of divine and cosmic order from the earth's natural features, we have an encyclopaedia of life-support systems where the natural ancestral ones are practically overcome (and mostly hidden) by the weight of those built on them by us for ourselves. Diagrams and energy flows replace genealogies. Inputs and outputs replace divine unions and their issue. But the genealogical sequence of evolution (of the emergence from Gaia of natural features and ultimately of all present life) as well as the primordial or 'deep time' timescale remain. Gaia theory uses contemporary scientific language to plot our evolutionary genealogy issuing from the union of organism and environment.

This contemporary presentation of the evolution of life on earth functions as a focus for thought; as a net of ideas and attitudes that guarantee our identity within the community of life on earth. What the salmon myth and others did, however, it fails to do directly. In its scientific form it consciously avoids teaching us about the existential reality of gift relationships within Gaia and our proper response to them: about living *as if* the gifts that support all life within the global environment are to be shared in ways that ensure their continuance for the good of all members of the earth community. Instead the sheer volume of scientific information now available on different aspects of our life-support systems has created a sense of heightened uncertainty about our role within Gaia – other than as a destructive force.

Perhaps because of this, physicist Freeman Dyson sees the re-personifying of the planet as Gaia (in my terms here, its mythologizing) as a hopeful sign of sanity in modern society. For him, the central complexity of human nature lies in our emotions, not in our intelligence. (Or perhaps, in the interaction between them.) Emotions, he says, belong to the group, to the family, to the tribe, to the species. They have a longer history and deeper roots than intelligence. An emotional bond with Gaia must, he says, be preserved, for '[R]espect for Gaia is the beginning of wisdom' (Primavesi 1998: 82). Surely anything that helps establish our identity as earth-centred rather than heaven-centred, as children of Gaia rather than sons of Zeus, must be considered helpful in responding to present environmental crises.

In this contemporary mythic context, UNESCO's call to include geology, geophysics, geochemistry, oceanography and atmospheric sciences under the heading of 'Earth Sciences' or 'knowledge resources for an understanding of our unique home in the universe' acquires a deeper significance. For taken together they show that:

[E]arth structure, climate, global cycles and biodiversity are all inter-related and operate as a single integrated earth system.... The earth orbits the sun at an optimal distance at which it is just warm enough for life to evolve. Living communities produce, consume and decompose energy foods made with the help of solar energy.... The earth system is an interaction between its nonliving, or abiotic part – comprised of rock, water and gases moving through geological stages of cooling, plate shifting and rock erosion – and the living organic world, or biotic part, that is comprised of bacteria, fungi, plants and animals. The atmosphere and oceans are chemically altered by organisms, and life has evolved to adapt itself to the local physical and chemical environment. *This part of what is now called 'Gaia theory' is now largely accepted.* This theory predicts that, in time, more evidence will emerge to demonstrate that life actually controls and fine-tunes the conditions of its environment for its own advantage.

(EOLSS 2002: 42. My italics)

Once again we are called to see ourselves as one species among many within the whole community of life on earth: to see ourselves as truly earth-centred. But to suppose (as the concluding sentence does) that science predicts that (human) life (for so it will be generally read) controls and fine-tunes the conditions of the global environment *for its own advantage* would run directly contrary to the basic premise of the theory and to the fact of increasing poverty and mortality rates among our most vulnerable brothers and sisters. For within a solely commodity exchange culture the advantage of the few, not of the many, is assured.

The images and language used in EOLSS are not those of the pre-industrial Northern Pacific tribes. Our built environment and commodity exchange culture has changed, if not almost totally occluded, our perception of those other living communities/tribes of bacteria, fungi, plants and animals on which we depend for food made with solar energy. What has *not* changed is the truth of our biological dependence on them and on continuous interaction between the biotic and the abiotic: between life and death within the whole earth system. And therefore, that we are no exception to the rules of self-regulation and interdependence that maintain the existential reality of Gaia's gift in a dynamic equilibrium.

This truth lay at the heart of the solar myths of earlier cultures as well as the salmon myths of the Northern Pacific tribes. They all presupposed an experience-based understanding of our interdependence with other living beings. The tribes knew that if the salmon did not come up the river to spawn many members of the tribe would die. They also believed that if they did not make a ritual return of the salmon to the sea the salmon's tribe too would die.

The return of the salmon was a gift: not something that could be controlled by the tribe, or by their possessions, or by their work; or even by the ritual itself. Just as the builders of Newgrange hailed the sun's return as an annual gift: one not subject to conditions imposed by them and not to be taken for granted.

The practice of gift exchange

The tribal ritual not only expressed gratitude for the gift of life from the sea. It also expressed thanks for the unquantifiable increase of life through that gift within the tribe and within each individual's life. Every member of the tribe consumed part of the salmon's flesh. Through and in its consumption a double truth about their life was discerned and acknowledged. First, the concrete, physical life of the tribe increased as the body of the gift was consumed. The flesh was 'used up' in this increase. But at the same time the tribe's social, emotional and spiritual life was also increased. 'Eating the gift' together they destroyed the salmon's life – and at the same time increased the quality of their own life with other members of the tribe.

The salmon's death was shown to increase life in the tribe in a variety of ways. Immense care was taken to ensure that the bones of the dead salmon would be preserved intact and returned to the sea. This meticulous concern not only acknowledged the liberality of the sea and of the salmon. The bones of the dead symbolized what does not die even when the body dies – in modern scientific terms, the constant interaction between the abiotic and the biotic: between the living and the dead. Out of that interaction the salmon will return. And the life of the tribe continue.

The actual giving of the food within the tribe affirmed goodwill to and from all its members as well as to and from the wider community of life. As the food passed from hand to hand, it became an agent of social cohesion and again led to the feeling that its sharing among them increased its worth. In this first circulation of the salmon as food the whole becomes greater than the sum of its parts. The gift increases in worth by bringing the group together. Not only that. The gift and its bearers share a spirit (of the generosity of life) which is kept alive by its motion among them. And so on until the bones are returned to the sea.

Hyde emphasizes that what he considers the core of the gift, the increase, comes as it moves from second to third party and even further. It does not lie in the simpler passage from first to second. The increase begins when the gift has passed *through* someone:

> Capital earns profit and the sale of a commodity turns a profit, but gifts that remain gifts do not *earn* profit, they *give* increase. The distinction lies in what we might call the vector of the increase: in gift exchange it,

the increase, stays in motion and follows the object, while in commodity exchange its stays behind as profit. . . . The increase that comes of gift exchange must remain a gift and not be kept as if it were the return on private capital. . . . To reverse the vector of the increase may not destroy its material portion (it may even augment it), but the social and spiritual portions drop away.

(Hyde 1999: 37f.)

So 'profit' is not the right word for this increase. To speak of the increase of gifts is to speak of something simultaneously material, social and spiritual – and therefore of a community, however small. The increase belongs to a body larger than that of any individual participant. So, Hyde says, a circulation of gifts nourishes those parts of our spirit that are not entirely personal: parts that derive from nature, the group, the race or the gods. Furthermore, although these wider spirits are part of us they are not 'ours': they are bestowed on us. 'To say, then, that the increase of a gift must itself be a gift is to ask that we not abandon the increase-of-the-whole in favour of a more individual and more plainly material growth' (Hyde 1999: 38).

When, however, we reverse the direction of the increase – when we profit on exchange or convert one man's gift to another's capital – we nourish that part of our being that is separate and distinct from others. Every age, Hyde says, must find its balance between the two. But is that possible today in a world where the myth of the free market appears to act as sole container for collective wisdom, requiring us, it seems, to accept the identity of consumers and find fulfilment in the purchase, use and display of consumables? It is only possible, I shall argue in the following chapter, if we are prepared to deepen our theoretical understanding of the existential reality of Gaia's gift by accepting its mythic as well as its scientific connotations. For that is the way in which we show recognition of the giver.

9 Gift exchange today

How does a deepening understanding of the existential reality of Gaia's gift help us to recognize its giver? And why would something so counter-cultural now appear possible within our sophisticated societies? The short answer is because now, as we saw in the preceding chapters, it is as much part of an ecological understanding as it is of a mythic one to see ourselves as participants in natural cycles. We are learning scientifically, and so socially and spiritually as well, that what we give to nature affects what nature gives to us – for good or ill. We are also learning that we cannot take that giving for granted: that making too many demands on life-support cycles upsets the balance between life and death within them and is ultimately lethal – for those life supports and therefore for us.

> [N]ature does things to *us* – it makes our crops grow and it destroys them, it provides what we need and frustrates our efforts to survive. It also responds to what we do to it; ecosystems are changed, the climate becomes more violent and unpredictable, nature behaves differently as a result of human activities.
>
> (Milton 2002: 82)

We now know that we are doing things to Gaia, the planetary life-support system, and that Gaia responds in different ways. The scale of that response, as well as our role in provoking it, is beginning to register. Human activities and technologies are seen to have global effects and ecosystem and climate change has become a major focus for scientific research. The United Nations plays a leading role in disseminating and correlating research results and in supporting non-governmental as well as governmental coalitions aimed at highlighting possible human responses to them. These initiatives, from the perspective of the preceding chapters, can be seen as an effort to reverse the human sense of separateness fostered by our seeing earth's gifts solely in terms of the material profit to be made from them.

But something deeper is necessary, something to drive home the sense of our connectedness that is for the most part left implicit in scientific research. We need to focus on the deep time period in earth's life history that precedes any present gift to us or our use of it. That helps us realize that long before we emerged to do things *to* Gaia, Gaia was doing things *for* us: things that would prove essential for our eventual emergence as a species and for our lives here and now. The support systems essential for our survival evolved over deep time through the synchrony of favourable conditions within three critical parameters: water availability, temperature and nutrient supply. These conditions and their continuance in a dynamic state of equilibrium were thought until quite recently (by those who did not attribute them directly to God) to be 'a happy accident'. Until, that is, James Lovelock studied them, their synchronicity and its subsequent effects.

He distinguished between the physical and chemical conditions that first allowed life to emerge, such as the presence of water, and those necessary for life's support *after* it had emerged. The chemistry and the climate of Earth would not, says, have persisted in a state favourable for life indefinitely. It was the evolution of the tightly coupled system, life *and* its environment, 'that sustained the small range of temperatures and chemical compositions that was and still is favourable for the persistence of life'. Once life began to change the atmosphere, the

> self-regulation of the earth's climate and chemistry then became a natural and inevitable consequence, or as the philosophers would say, it became an 'emergent' property of the system. Emergent because the entire system when working had properties absent from a mere collection of all the component parts.
>
> (Lovelock 1991: 74–84)

This entire system, this totality, is what Lovelock calls 'Gaia'. The part we have played and now play within it necessarily affects it in its entirety. There is no question of our being exempted from the effects of its self-regulation, for good or ill. Nor can we exempt ourselves from contributing to them, for good or ill. In that sense, we all do things to Gaia and Gaia does things to us. And those things cannot be properly seen or judged other than in the context of the whole and over timescales beyond our usual reckoning. However for the first time in Gaia's history, or in human history, the effects of human activities on ourselves as well as on our environment are forcing themselves on our attention. We are slowly learning how to take account, as far as we can, of what we do to Gaia and what Gaia does to us.

Indeed our increasing ability to do this is part of Gaia's theoretical and conceptual gift to us. But thinking about what Gaia does *for* us elicits other equally necessary and valid responses. Being aware of the greater whole within which we live arouses feelings and emotional responses, such as Darwin's awe, Huxley's admiration as well as Volk's and Sagan's gratitude that are not anthropological curiosities but a necessary part of human reactions to the world. The emotional impact Nature makes on us is also part of its meaning for us, part of 'the grasp I have on the world' (Weil 1987: 48–55). And meanings give things their value. We value things by perceiving meanings in them and these meanings literally 'make themselves *felt*' (Milton 2002: 100. My italics).

So the process of valuing Gaia's gift for making my existence possible, or of finding meaning in scientific theories that explain how it does so, is inseparable from the emotions it induces in me. For the North Pacific tribes the return of the salmon meant the renewal of life and the gratitude that aroused in them enhanced that meaning and drove them to express it in communal rituals.

All this harks back to what I said in Chapter 8 about the function of myth. It acts like a collective container for imagination, thought, emotions, meanings and a certain shared perception of, or grasp on, the world. But how do we express those thoughts and emotions that belong to a shared perception of earth as providing the gifts of life and of death?

Symbol and myth

This is where mythic expressions of Gaia theory play an important role. Before her name was given to a theory that stirs the intellectual passion of scientists and the rational imagination of our age, Gaia, the primal earth deity, was held sacred: seen as beloved of the gods and as holder of life and death for all. Paul Ricoeur quotes a mythic Homeric hymn that celebrates her as follows:

> Solid earth, beloved of the gods, who nourished everything in the world . . . you are the one who gives life to mortal beings and who takes it away again.
>
> (Ricoeur 1995: 53)

This perception of earth and her role in our lives was not, of course, confined to premodern western culture. Ricoeur quotes a Hindu Rig Veda funeral ritual that says: 'You who are earth, I place on the earth.' In contemporary Christian rituals earth is often sprinkled on the coffin by mourners. At such moments we 'act out' the belief that Earth gives us life and receives it back again from us in death. And, for some people, giving a token handful of soil back to earth at the moment when death appears most final expresses the hope that life will emerge again from that death in some form or other.

These symbolic expressions of feeling, perception and emotion, in which a handful of earth stands for an individual's life and death, are integral to the mythic understanding of Gaia. Ricoeur's connection between myth and symbol makes this clear. He insists that in a myth of the sacred universe (such as that of Gaia), there are not a few living beings here and there, but 'life is a total and diffuse sacrality that may be seen in the cosmic rhythms, in the return of vegetation and in the alternation of life and death' (Ricoeur 1995: 52).

These physical phenomena are what he calls 'the configurations of the cosmos'. Therefore whatever symbols are used in 'performing' the myth are 'bound' to express and articulate those configurations. In regard to death, they manifest the renewal of life on earth that we see in the return of vegetation and that is, we know, as much part of the structure of the physical universe as of the mythic or sacred one.

I want to unwrap this particular kind of structural physical coupling integral to myth and symbol as parallel, or configured to the systemic bonding between life and environment presupposed by Gaia theory. Where Lovelock offers the concept of 'self-regulation' as an emergent property of the entire system, Ricoeur offers the word 'sacred'. This property of Gaia was explored at some length in the closing chapters of *Sacred Gaia* where I argued that sacredness attaches to totalities, to 'wholes' that we tinker with at our peril (Primavesi 2000: 168f.). For Ricoeur the emergent property of total and diffuse sacrality in life can only be conveyed in symbols that express and articulate the physical, material bonds that support life. Therefore the logic of meaning in myth, the logic that binds symbol and myth together, 'proceeds from the very structure of the sacred universe'. In other words, as the meaning cannot be separated out from the whole, so too what we call 'the sacred' cannot be assigned to one part and not to another. From this perspective all is sacred, or nothing is. For everything is sacred when seen in the context of life as a 'total and diffuse sacrality'.

Ricoeur explains that the logic that binds symbol and myth together works through 'a law of *correspondences*', that is, the symbols correspond to some visible aspect of the universe. He names four types of correspondence.

The first is that between the order of natural appearances (the sky) and what we call 'celestial' or heavenly – in other words, that which is 'above' us. This symbolic correspondence has been a recurrent theme throughout this book.

The second is that between the macrocosm and the microcosm – the union of earth and sky is taken to correspond to that of female and male. Both symbolic correspondences are a regular feature in Christian representations of the notion of 'mystical marriage' within Christianity. Numerous paintings of St Catherine of Siena depict her gazing upwards as she is pierced by a beam of light. Similarly the many paintings of St Sebastian's martyrdom found in European churches show his gaze fixed on heaven as he is pierced by arrows.

The third correspondence is that between the furrowed earth and the female genital organ; between the entrails of the earth and the maternal womb; between the sun and the eye (Apollo's eye); between semen and seed grain; between burial and the death of grain; between birth and the return of springtime. These symbolic resonances persist, as ecofeminists have noted, not only because of their correspondence with the visible physical realities of agriculture and of human physiology, but also because of their faithful correspondence to gendered power structures, political, social and linguistic, within patriarchal societies (Merchant 1980: 1–41; Primavesi 1991: 32–36).

The fourth correspondence (and this takes us back to the imagery in Copernicus's Preface and to the architecture of Newgrange) is that found in three registers: the body, the house and the cosmos. This makes the pillars of a temple and the spinal column, the roof of a house and the skull, the proportions of the body and of the universe, all mutually signify one another. It also makes thresholds, gates, bridges and narrow pathways correspond to homologous 'passages' at critical moments in the human life journey such as birth, puberty, marriage and death.

In all of these correspondences, whatever symbol is used (such as seed falling into earth, soil thrown on a coffin or bones into the sea) 'is bound to the configuration of the cosmos'. In other words, it corresponds to what occurs naturally. Symbolism is *significant*, that is, it bears a range of meanings 'only when borne by the sacred valences of the elements themselves'. These sacred valences may be seen, as Ricoeur says, in the cosmic rhythms, in the return of vegetation (or the sun, or salmon) and in the alternation of life and death (Ricoeur 1995: 52–55).

Walt Whitman expresses this more simply when he speaks of 'the truth of earth', a truth that literally and figuratively grounds his own poetic symbolism. The central symbol in his poetry, 'leaves of grass', almost always refers to 'grass over graves'. Because for him earth's truth corresponds to the fact that forms of life perish – but rise again out of their own decay. Grass is 'the beautiful uncut hair of graves'. And as the grass is food for animal life, so we animals, with the death of the body, become food for grass (Hyde 1999: 178–182).

In the poem 'Compost' Whitman brings this earthly truth into correspondence with the truth about ourselves. The title announces the uncompromising correspondence between earthly life and earthly decay in the macrocosm (earth) and the microcosm (us):

> The resurrection of the wheat appears with pale visage out of its
>   graves...
> Now I am terrified at the Earth! It is that calm and patient,
> It grows such sweet things out of such corruptions...
> It gives such divine materials to men, and accepts such leavings from
>   them at last.

(Whitman 1926: 286–288)

His authentic feeling of terror at the evidence of this truth remains part of a proper reaction to it. Earth can and does terrify us even as we perceive what it does to us and for us. Small wonder that we want to stifle such feelings. Yet they remind us that we do not, ultimately, have a choice about living *as if* we are members of the whole earth community. There is no question of our being simply observers of it. If grass is food for us, so we are food for grass. This uncomfortable truth lies at the heart of true gift exchange. It focuses uncompromisingly on what it is that makes the gift of life possible for us: the ceaseless chemistry of exchange between death and life that is the 'givenness' of food.

The concept of givenness

In the philosophical debate about gift exchange the concept of 'givenness' (*Gegebenheit*) refers to prior conditions that make gift exchange possible. I am using it here to refer to antecedent conditions within deep time and before human history that I neither created nor contributed to, but that were and are essential for my existence. In short, it refers here to the 'givenness' of Gaia, to its support for all life and eventually, for human life. And of course, to the role played by death in that support.

Philosophically, 'givenness' is presupposed in order to account for the creation of an excess without which a gift cannot be (freely) given. Givenness signifies an abundance within the system, a surplus or excess that necessarily precedes any actual exchange of gifts. In regard to the greatest gift, life, how is that excess created? Through the lives, labour and deaths of countless other beings coupled tightly with earth throughout and since deep time. They pro-created the increase, the abundance through which those that came after them could live, incorporating the potential of the gift to both perish and give increase (see the beginning of Chapter 5). From this perspective I understand rather better Sagan's remark that the evolution (of life) is powered by change and death.

The presence of 'givenness' within myself too, my own ability to give, also flows from procreative interactions between beings who lived before me (most obviously my biological ancestors) and 'gave' birth to me. From that givenness, other types of gift exchange, individual, communal and cultural, became possible and enriched my physical, moral, social and spiritual existence. They created within me the potential for giving something (whether of myself or outside of myself) freely to others without any expectation of return. *What* I give, and to whom, will be decided by the quality of attention I pay to those around me. Indeed, that attention may itself be the greatest gift I can offer them. In particular, being attentive to what it means for someone else to be alive means being attentive to their wellbeing but, above all, to their suffering and to its causes. And that in turn means being attentive to the effects of my own actions – on those nearest to me in time, space and relationships but, ultimately, to their effects on Gaia as a whole.

The philosophical debate about the nature of givenness concentrates on its necessarily preceding any inter-human gift exchange. That debate does not, however, as far as I am aware, pay attention to the 'deep time' conditions that, in the course of evolutionary history, gave our species the gift of life and made it possible for us to give life in return. This primary 'givenness' is taken as 'given': for atheists, as a 'happy accident' (Caputo 1999: 65–71). So the discussion centres on the undoubted fact that the possibility of any true gift exchange between us lies in a 'given' that is prior to the gift itself. (The discussion proceeds from there, as we shall see, to the question of who the 'giver' of that 'givenness' might be.)

I want to draw attention here to something that the practice of gift exchange among the Northern Pacific tribes clearly showed. When the givenness of life is particularized into *what* is given to keep us alive here and now, the salmon, then the 'givenness' of the sea and all it incorporates is intuitively perceived as necessarily preceding the gift of the salmon. So the value of that givenness and its meaning for the tribe's life is symbolically articulated in ritual. The affluence built up throughout and through the sea's existence is discerned as essential for the salmon to appear – either as a living being, or as a gift, or as both. This affluence, the ritual affirms, was not created, earned or paid for by those who benefit from it, whether humans, birds, or brown bears. So the salmon bones are returned to the sea. Consciously or not, this manifests the desire to contribute to as well as to maintain in some measure the conditions of 'givenness'. Those conditions are beyond the control of those who benefit from them. They belong to the totality of the sea and not to any one part of it or any being within it. What the myth says, the ritual performs.

Writing now about the practice and meaning of those ceremonies, our distance from them can be measured not only in years or by forgotten rituals but in ever-decreasing numbers of wild salmon; in the worsening quality of life among those who live off marine ecosystems; in the worldwide depletion of fish stocks through factory fishing and in the near extinction of some seabirds (such as albatross and petrel) who die when caught on the millions of baited hooks set in long line fishing. Our commodity exchange culture takes the 'givenness' of both fish and birds for granted. Yet our increasing knowledge of the chemistry between natural cycles that produces such stocks of 'natural capital' informs us that the abundance, the inherent quality of givenness in the whole, is produced by more than the sum of its parts. In Lovelock's terms, this givenness is an emergent property of the entire Gaian system. It is neither quantifiable nor completely observable. Nor are we able to capture in words or equations the mysterious, elusive, synchronous conjunction of factors (such as the 'dead matter' we call marine snow) that 'gives' us this marine life-support system.

What I have said about the givenness of the sea can, of course, equally well be said about the soil and its gifts. Or about the atmosphere. Or about the chemistry between all of these that makes up the givenness of the systems that gives us food to keep us alive and able to exchange gifts. The information on these systems comes now in a seemingly endless and often contradictory stream from scientific research projects worldwide. But it requires more than intellectual assent from us.

We need to recognize and respond to both aspects of Gaia's gift. According to our temperament, education and culture, we shall probably find one aspect more compelling than the other. *Both*, however, are needed. We need rational, logical science to help us understand the givenness of being alive on earth today *and* 'irrational' religion, myth, ritual and poetry to respond ritually to our experience of it. Together they create a balanced and effective response.

The cultural perception of givenness today

When considering today's declining fish stocks, the coherence of emotion and reason that appears to have informed the salmon myth and tribal responses to it shows up the deficiencies of rational analysis alone. It also exposes the difficulty within a consumerist commodity culture of supplementing scientific analysis with practices based on an intuitive perception of givenness. Mythical or ritual expressions of gratitude to 'the planet on the table' have no place in this culture. Indeed, the table itself, as the ritual space for meals and for the shared life of the household, has practically disappeared. For food and drink is routinely carried around house or street in disposable containers until consumed – when the containers are thrown away. The 'givenness' of their contents is traced, if at all, no further than the fast food outlet, the household fridge or, ultimately, the cash till.

This consumerist culture is not defined by the fact that we all necessarily 'consume' food. It is defined by the conspicuous consumption (and waste) of the widest possible range of consumables – available to those who can pay for them. It is defined by the rising number of famine victims proportionate to the commodification, packaging and over-production of consumables within the 'free' market. The visible and ubiquitous symbol of the consumerist myth is the concept, invocation and ritual use of 'fast' food:

> The fast-food industry today is dominated by the products of industrial processing, designed to be eaten 'on the fly' or in front of television or computer screen. Instead of a bond, meals are becoming a barrier. 'Convenience' enjoys a higher priority than civilisation or pleasure or nourishment.
>
> (Fernandez-Armesto 2001: 248f.)

The visible effects of consumerist practice on the consumers themselves appear in such apparently disparate phenomena as a growth in both the incidence of obesity *and* of anorexia. The less visible but equally if not more alarming increase in the size of our ecological footprint is evident in depleted natural resources accompanied by larger and larger amounts of waste products. The larger the mound, the deeper the pit needed to accommodate it. So tax laws are introduced to raise revenue to dig larger pits and to hide their contents from view and from our consciousness. 'Composting' is, at best, a private, not a collective response to what cannot be or is not consumed by us – whether packaging or bones. All this reinforces as well as follows from the presuppositions of a predominantly cash exchange commodity culture.

At best they blur, at worst they obliterate any perception of food as a gift dependent on earth's givenness. Although without reference to consumerist culture, philosopher Jean-Luc Marion describes the state of affairs within it in regard to givenness:

> We can imagine and say that something is given and appears as given without referring it to another thing or being or object that would be the cause of its givenness. It is very important to understand that you can describe a phenomenon as given without asking any question about the giver. And in most of the cases, there is absolutely no [perceived] giver at all.
>
> (Caputo 1999: 70)

Although this is not his declared intention, Marion points here to the 'invisibility' of the provider, the earth, that makes ritual responses to the givenness of food almost impossible. This invisibility corresponds to, indeed results from, what I have called the 'distance' between the consumer/ purchaser, the commodity itself and its natural resource base. The distance is compounded by an advertising industry that focuses attention on the brand and so on the product, usually without any reference to that natural resource base. And as availability is seen to depend on one's ability to pay, the 'givenness' of nature disappears totally from view.

Sometimes, however, there is a perverted sort of acknowledgment of the effects of our purchasing power. Shortly after writing the above paragraph, a half-page newspaper advertisement for an upmarket store caught my eye. It showed a large expanse of blue sky and water bisected by the dark line of a narrow pathway. This focused attention on an emaciated, dejected looking brown bear exiting to the right of the picture. Taped high to the left above him was the message: '*a Harvey Nichols Food-Fashion Victim. Fresh Wild Salmon*' (*Guardian* 28 September 2002: 28. My italics).

The human-engineered consumerist system operates as if the givenness of global life-support systems exists solely for the satisfaction of human-manufactured temporary 'needs' – such as having, wearing, buying or eating the latest fashion. It presupposes a human right to consume that destroys rather than increases that givenness. The energy, minerals, air, water, soil and species that contribute to it are considered human possessions – at best to be used for the good of as many people as possible. Culturally it presupposes the doctrine of human exceptionalism in regard to life and what supports it: just as the religious form of the doctrine did in regard to death.

Religious perceptions of givenness today

Marion rightly cautions us against thinking that today there is, or that there is not, a 'giver' who can or cannot be named without further ado. Consequently he discusses what 'givenness' might mean, or might be, by warning us (again rightly) that:

> When they [gifts] appear to us as given, of course, we have to receive them, but that does not imply that we should claim God as the cause of what we receive.
>
> (Caputo 1999: 70)

That claim, however, remains one of the fundamental religious teachings in the ongoing story, or should I say predominant religious myth about earth, ourselves and God. Picking up the narrative thread for one last time, a literal translation of the Hebrew text of Genesis says that after the Flood and the ritual slaughter of some 'clean' animals, God was 'pleased' and spoke as follows to Noah and to his sons:

> Be fruitful, increase, fill the earth
> Fear of you, terror of you
> Shall be upon all the beasts of the earth
> All the fowl of the skies
> All that creeps on the ground
> All the fish of the sea
> They are given into your hand
> Every creeper that lives shall be for you for eating
> As the green of plants
> I give all to you.
>
> (Korsak 1993: 33)

'I give *all* to you' – except, of course, the life of any human being made in God's image.

Marion warns us that 'givenness', as the prior condition for and cause of our receiving gifts, should not be immediately or directly attributed to God. I agree with the intent behind his warning, that is, that the concept of God should not be reduced to that of a source or dispenser of gifts. And that it is theologically unsound to explain, on behalf of God, what God's purposes in creating givenness might be. It is not just, as Marion says, that we lack intuitions concerning God. We lack concepts fitting God.

However I see the theological problem rather differently. Not only do we lack intuitions about God. We lack primary intuitions about ourselves and about our earth-centredness – and, necessarily, full knowledge of God's purposes. So we lack intuitions about what earth's 'givenness' means for the total and diffuse sacrality of life on earth. That narrows our perception of that meaning down to what it means for us. And when this primary intuition of the 'truth of earth', of earth's givenness in our lives, is lacking, stunted or ignored, so is the possibility of any meaningful religious ritual response to it. The religious option traditionally offered Christians is to refer our inchoate gratitude for earth's gifts (usually symbolized by bread and wine) directly to God. And they are (usually) shared only with those considered worthy (by those who say they represent God) to receive them.

I went into this type of discriminatory practice in regard to the Eucharist at some length in *Our God Has No Favourites: A Liberation Theology of the Eucharist* (1989). In it I compared present-day Eucharistic rituals (unfavourably) with the open table fellowship recorded of Jesus, in which he was castigated for dining with those considered 'unclean' in the eyes of religious observers. Pictures from famine-torn societies remind us, I said, that for the hungry, food forces itself on their attention as an insistent symbol of life sustained or destroyed. But our consumer-glutted society keeps us safely at one remove from hunger's savage insistence. Hunger is a forgotten feeling. Here to eat well means to eat less. And to live well no longer implies sharing food or hospitality with others, since it is assumed they can provide for themselves or, if not, that there are organizations, state-funded or otherwise, who will look after them.

This has led to a loss of the essential correspondence between the ritual meal of bread and wine and the role played by food, and by its sharing, in our lives. The invitation to share in the Eucharist is extended only to those 'in good standing' with the ecclesiastical authorities. Therefore it loses the unconditional character of Jesus's table fellowship and becomes a symbol of church power, corresponding to that exercised in including or excluding others from membership on grounds laid down by ecclesiastical authorities who see that power, ultimately, as determining who lives forever in heaven. It no longer corresponds (although in certain cases it may) to who lives and dies on earth (Primavesi and Henderson 1989: 11–13). And if that is how we ritualize our eating with co-religionists, not to mention our fellow-humans, what chance is there of our seeing the sharing of food as a matter of justice towards the whole community of life on earth? If God has given *all* to us, then emaciated bears and other victims of consumerist fashion can be and are used as cruel endorsements of that claim.

This means that any religious perception of earth's 'givenness' as intended for any being other than us, is ignored, indeed lost. No real sense of gratitude for the gifts earth gives is either felt or expressed. Instead Gaia's gift is seen as earned: either directly from human suppliers or religiously, as a reward from God for good conduct, for 'pleasing' God. Gratitude for what earth freely gives is transferred on to other people or on to God. Either way our perspective on Gaia's givenness and on those whose creative labours contribute to it is foreshortened to a view of ourselves alone and our relationship with God. Earth is overlooked to the point that its given-ness effectively disappears from view. The possibility of seeing Gaia's gift as freely given, without thought or expectation of return, is lost. Instead, our return of thanks to God for Gaia's gift is conceived of as earning an eternal reward in heaven: conditional on our 'good' behaviour *on* earth – but not *towards* earth.

From such a perspective, what earth itself has given and continues to give to countless other life forms, and what it means to us and to our lives, is lit-erally, religiously and imaginatively discounted. This worldview teaches us, indeed constrains us to ignore what we are now slowly and painfully learn-ing about our earth-centredness: that without earth's givenness built up over deep time, and without the present gifts of life-support systems made possible by it, we would not exist, could not exist. And that if we do not preserve, respect and nourish that givenness, Gaia's gift to us, although not necessarily to those who come after us, will fail.

> Great is the Earth, and the way it became what it is:
> Do you imagine it has stopped at this? the increase abandoned?
> Understand then that it goes as far onward from this as this is from the times when it lay in covering waters and gases, before man had appeared . . .
> O truth of the earth! O truth of things! I am determined to press my way toward you.
>
> (Whitman 1926: 269–271)

Notes

1 I shall use the Latin term *homocentric* for 'man-centred' rather than the more usual Greek derivative *anthropocentric* because (a) Copernicus wrote in Latin and used this term and (b) *homo* can be used inclusively, and perhaps more correctly in his case, to describe the human race; just as 'man' was used colloquially in English until recently. However *homo* also signifies a male individual, *vir*, as opposed to a female, *femina* or *mulier*. And given our present awareness of the gendered nature of society in general I feel it expresses more precisely the male-specific character of the social and religious culture in Copernicus's day. The other term I shall use frequently, *geocentric*, earth-centred, is not so culturally charged, although, as we shall see, it does allow for different emphases in interpretation. The use of *heliocentric*, or sun-centred, remains unambiguous.

2 Heiko Oberman goes to great pains to rebut Thomas Kuhn's assertion that Luther, Calvin and Melanchthon led the way in citing Scripture against Copernicus and urged repression of Copernicans (Oberman 1986).

3 In a review of *Sacred Gaia*, theologian/scientist Christopher Southgate used the same argument, almost verbatim. In response to my call for theology to take Darwin seriously he wrote that 'Darwinian schemes' [sic] can certainly not rule out a particular *theological* (as opposed to biological) status for humans' (Southgate 2001).

4 Implicit in Gingerich's analysis is a general question about the nature of our responses to what we perceive: about the kind of emotions, judgements and assertions it arouses in us and that, pictorially, colours it for us. Arne Naess uses the term 'apperceptive gestalt' to describe the complex character of our perceptions, their interactions with other elements of the self, such as our emotions or our judgement, and their role in binding 'the I and the not-I together in a whole'. Gestalt formation crosses boundaries between what is conventionally classed as thinking as separated from emotion (Naess 1989).

5 Michael Polanyi claims that the intellectual passion that informs scientific discovery (and informed the three scientists in question) does not merely affirm the existence of relationships that foreshadow an indeterminate range of future discoveries. Scientific discovery has other effects that Polanyi calls its creative work: creative because it changes the world as we see it by deepening our understanding of it. The change, he says, is irrevocable. Having made such a discovery, I shall never see the world, or myself, as I did before. The cumulative creative effect of the work of Copernicus, Darwin and Lovelock may yet, then, change our perception of our own importance.

Polanyi's discussion of 'heuristic passion' and the consequent 'fruitfulness' of Copernicanism is very much to the point here (Polanyi 1958; Primavesi 1998).

6 They are not alone in this. Roger Penrose stresses the fact that 'Gödel's theorem tells us that there are aspects of our understanding which you cannot encompass in a computational picture' and that 'nature has been a lot cleverer than physics has been able to be so far, but why not?' (Penrose 2002).

Philosopher of science Paul Feyerabend, one of the most consistent critics of science's truth claims, commented that Galileo identified the natural interpretations inconsistent with Copernicus and replaced them with new ones (such as the relativity of all motion and the law of circular inertia) formulated in a new and highly abstract observation language. However, Galileo offers no *theoretical* reasons why the telescope should be expected to give a true picture of the sky. Nor did the initial experience with the telescope provide such reasons (Feyerabend 1993). I am grateful to Edward James for drawing these two examples to my attention.

7 This touches on a large and growing area of debate and as a useful introduction to its practical and theoretical aspects I would recommend *Wolves and Human Communities*, Sharpe, Norton and Donnelley (eds); *Unsanctifying Human Life*, a collection of Peter Singer's writings edited and with a comprehensive introduction by Helga Kuhse; *Animals and Why They Matter*, by Mary Midgley; *The Gnat is Older than Man*, by Christopher Stone.

8 Livio quotes the twelfth-century Jewish philosopher Moses Maimonides: 'Man is composed of body and mind, and all his modes of behaviour are either forms of motion, which constitutes the action of his body, or forms of knowing, which constitutes the action of his mind' (Livio 2000). See also Descartes: 'We clearly conceive mind, that is, a substance which thinks, without body, that is to say, without an extended substance; and, on the other hand, we as clearly conceive body without mind (as everyone [sic] admits)' (Descartes 1912).

This supposed/imposed dichotomy within the self (between mind and body) has greatly preoccupied philosophers, psychiatrists, poets and phenomenologists among others. As usually understood it has supported the common presupposition that rationality is either unconnected with, or at least superior to, bodiliness, and above all, to animality/earthiness. Ecofeminist theorists such as Carolyn Merchant are particularly exercised by this, as women have long been associated with bodiliness/earthiness and men with mind/rationality (Merchant (1980) *The Death of Nature: Women, Ecology and the Scientific Revolution*. New York, NY, Harper and Row; Plumwood (1993) *Feminism and the Mastery of Nature*. London and New York, NY, Routledge; Sturgeon (1997) *Ecofeminist Natures: Race, Gender, Feminist Theory and Political Action*. London, Routledge).

They find that such a degrading distinction (which is what it is) reciprocally degrades women and earth since (within our cultural history) earth has routinely been conceptualized as female.

9 Bremmer gives what he calls a 'history' of the concept of soul among the Greeks, the Jews and the early Christians (McDannell and Lang 2001; Bremmer 2002).

10 It is interesting to note the effect this teaching subsequently had on women's lives. When it became possible during the early nineteenth century

for anaesthetics to be given to women in childbirth, there were violent objections on the grounds that they were *meant* to suffer pain as the consequence of 'original' sin. Queen Victoria did women a great service when she ordered anaesthesia in childbirth for herself and made its use respectable.

11 I am encouraged to expose this particular piece of theological plumbing by John Stuart Mill's comment over 150 years ago:

> On religion in particular the time appears to me to have come, when it is the duty of all who, being qualified in point of knowledge, have on mature consideration satisfied themselves that the current opinions are not only false but hurtful, to make their dissent known.
>
> (Hartshorne 1997)

12 Jeffrey Burton Russell, in his study *The History of Heaven*, traces the Christian idea of heaven back to Jewish and Greco-Roman culture where death was originally the door to a tenuous continued existence in the shadowy insubstantial region of Hades. One of the most beautiful and enduring evocations of this in art and music is the story of Orpheus's journey to the underworld to find Eurydice. Later, Russell says, the underworld became a happier place (this is evident in the frescoes in Etruscan tombs) as the belief that all the dead souls became shadows gradually shifted to the pious view that heroes – the virtuous and noble, loved by the gods – would have better lives than others in the future world. Philo's concept of the 'heavenly body' able to enjoy its delights fits into this framework as does Jesus's 'joy in heaven' and indeed Hardy's vision of Paradise as a 'glad' place.

The fact too that the underworld (that is, the under*ground*) was the source of gold and jewels was taken to signify that no gross matter persists in the realm of the blessed dead but only what is pure. And as crops pushed their way from below earth up into the sun, the underworld also symbolized the possibility of rebirth. The Greco-Roman notion that the happy fields of the blessed dead recapitulate a golden age free from war, famine and other evils can be seen, Russell said, to parallel the Jewish idea that the kingdom of God will come at the end of time and recapitulate the Paradise garden of Eden. A Paradise to which Muslims also aspire.

The contemporary Christian concept of heaven is, then, essentially Jewish in idea and image but influenced by Greco-Roman and other cultures, including prehistoric ones. The happy life of the blest in the classical Elysian Fields or Isles of the Just was modelled on that of an ideal earthly existence, one merited by their actions during their earthly life journey. Christians assimilated the idea of 'meriting' heaven by combining the Roman model of patriotism and heroism with the Jewish model of faithfulness to the Covenant. Even more easily assimilated (for Christianity began its life in the Roman Empire as largely the religion of slaves) was the Stoic idea (as against that of Roman nobility) that we are judged not by our social rank but by our virtuous practice (Russell 1997).

This democratizing of heaven has often been a positive imaginative force in the lives of those without economic, military or political power who must struggle for justice on earth.

Some of the earliest vernacular literary accounts of exemplary human journeys from birth to death, from earth to heaven, are found in Old English and Old Irish narratives. They use a wealth of images and metaphors that resonate with a historic and geographical reality, including the Old English *uplyft* (upper air or sky), *ceaster* (fort, city), *heofonham* (heaven-house), *heofonheall* (great hall or court of heaven), *heofonsetl* (residence or throne), *wuldorthrymm* (glory-majesty), *wuldordream* (glory-delight) (ibid.).

In Old Irish there is a collection of *immrama*, or ocean voyages, where the geography of the imagination and that of the physical landscape combine wonderfully. Thirty-one islands are visited in *Immram Curaig Maile Duin*, one more marvellous than another. On the islands and in the open sea the travellers encounter prodigies, accounts of which display considerable imaginative power and a nice sense of humour. Some islands figure as visions of hell, some of heaven: the former to be escaped from at all costs, the latter affording every delight of body and soul (Dillon 1994).

13 The effects of this cycle on European workers was graphically described by Simone Weil. See Primavesi (2000).

Bibliography

Abbott, W.M. (1966) *The Documents of Vatican II*. London and Dublin, Geoffrey Chapman.

Agamben, G. (1995) *Homo Sacer: Sovereign Power and Bare Life*. Stanford, CT, Stanford University Press.

Allan, S. (1997) *The Way of Water and Sprouts of Virtue*. New York, NY, State University of New York Press.

Altcappenberg, H.-T.S. (2000) *Sandro Botticelli: The Drawings for Dante's Divine Comedy*. London, Royal Academy of Arts.

Baldwin, J. (1990) *Notes of a Native Son*. Boston, MA, Beacon Press.

Barrow, J.D. and Tipler, Frank J. (1986) *The Anthropic Cosmological Principle*. Oxford, Oxford University Press.

Beer, G.P.K. (2000) *Darwin's Plots*. Cambridge, Cambridge University Press.

Berry, T. (1990) The Spirituality of the Earth. In *Liberating Life*, C. Birch, William Eakin and Jay B. McDaniel (eds). New York, NY, Orbis Books: 151–158.

Blumenberg, H. (1987) *The Genesis of the Copernican World*. Cambridge, MA, The MIT Press.

Brecht, B. (1980) *Life of Galileo*. London, Methuen.

Bremmer, J.N. (2002) *The Rise and Fall of the Afterlife*. London and New York, NY, Routledge.

Brennan, E. (ed.) (1990) *Heritage: A Visitor's Guide*. Dublin, Office of Public Works.

Caputo, J.D. and Scanlan, M.J. (eds) (1999) *God, the Gift, and Postmodernism*. Bloomington, IN, Indiana University Press.

Carse, J.P. (1994) *Breakfast at the Victory: The Mysticism of Ordinary Experience*. San Francisco, CA, Harper.

Chen, E. (1989). *The Tao Te Ching: A New Translation with Commentary*. St Paul, MN, Paragon House.

Clark, J.M. (1957) *Meister Eckhart: An Introduction to the Study of His Works, with an Anthology of His Sermons*. London, Nelson.

Cleary, T. (1993) *The Essential Tao*. New York, NY, HarperCollins.

Copernicus, N. (1992) *On the Revolutions of the Heavenly Spheres*. Baltimore, MD, The Johns Hopkins University Press.

Cosgrove, D. (2001) *Apollo's Eye: A Cartographic Genealogy of the Earth in Western Imagination*. Baltimore, MD, Johns Hopkins University Press.

cummings, e.e. (1960) *Selected Poems*. London, Faber.

Descartes, R. (1912) *A Discourse on Method*. London, J.M. Dent.

Dillenberger, J. (1988) *Protestant Thought and Natural Science: A Historical Interpretation*. Notre Dame, IN, University of Notre Dame Press.

Dillon, M. (1994) *Early Irish Literature*. Dublin, Four Courts Press.

EOLSS (2002) *An Illustrative and Informative Booklet produced for the launch of the Encyclopedia of Life Support Systems (EOLSS) at the World Summit on Sustainable Development (WSSD)*, Johannesburg, South Africa. EOLSS is a web-based archive accessible by subscription at www.eolss.net.

Fernandez-Armesto, F. (2001) *Food: A History*. London, Macmillan.

Feyerabend, P. (1993) *Against Method*. London, Verso.

Gingerich, O. (1975) Swerdlow's Analysis. In *The Copernican Achievement*, R. Westman (ed.). Berkeley, CA, University of California Press: 99–104.

Goodenough, U. (1998) *The Sacred Depths of Nature*. New York, NY and Oxford, Oxford University Press.

Gould, S.J. (1987) *Time's Arrow, Time's Cycle: Myth and Metaphor in the Discovery of Geological Time*. Cambridge, MA, Harvard University Press.

Gould, S.J. (2000) Time Scales and the Year 2000. In *Conversations about the End of Time*, C. David (ed.). London, Penguin: 1–44, 217–219.

Griffith-Dickson, G. (2000) *Human and Divine: An Introduction to the Philosophy of Religious Experience*. London, Duckworth.

Guthrie, S. (1993) *Faces in the Clouds: A New Theory of Religion*. New York, NY and Oxford, Oxford University Press.

Hallyn, F. (1997) *The Poetic Structure of the World: Copernicus and Kepler*. New York, NY, Zone Books.

Hardy, T. (1978) *Collected Poems*. London, Penguin Books.

Hartshorne, C. (1997) *The Zero Fallacy and Other Essays in Neoclassical Philosophy*. Chicago and La Salle, IL, Open Court.

Harvey, G. (2001) *The Forgiveness of Nature: The Story of Grass*. London, Jonathan Cape.

Hyde, L. (1999) *The Gift: Imagination and the Erotic Life of Property*. London, Random House.

Hynes, P. (1989) *The Recurring Silent Spring*. New York, NY and Oxford, Pergamon Press.

Jones, W.T. (1969) *Hobbes to Hume: A History of Western Philosophy*. New York, NY, Harcourt Brace Jovanich, Inc.

Kant, I. (1924) *Critique of Pure Reason*. London, Bell and Sons Ltd.

Korsak, M.P. (1993) *At the Start: Genesis Made New*. New York, NY, Doubleday.

Koyré, A. (1957) *From the Closed World to the Infinite Universe*. Baltimore, MD, Johns Hopkins University Press.

Koyré, A. (1973) *The Astronomical Revolution: Copernicus, Kepler, Borelli*. London, Methuen.

Kuhn, T. (1957) *The Copernican Revolution: Planetary Astronomy in the Development of Western Thought*. Cambridge, MA, Harvard University Press.

142   Bibliography

Lakatos, I. and Zahar, E. (1975) Why Did Copernicus' Research Programme Supersede Ptolemy's? In *The Copernican Achievement*, R. Westman (ed.). Berkeley, CA, University of California Press: 354–383.

Lear, L. (1997) *Rachel Carson: The Life of the Author of Silent Spring*. London, Allen Lane, the Penguin Press.

Lenton, T.M. (2002) Testing Gaia: The Effect of Life on Earth's Habitability. *Climatic Change*, Dordrecht, the Netherlands, Kluwer: 52, 409–422.

Lenton, T.M. (in press) Clarifying Gaia: Regulation With or Without Natural Selection. In *Scientists on Gaia: the Next Century*, S.H. Schneider, P.J. Boston and J. Miller (eds). London, MIT Press.

Levi, P. (1985) *The Periodic Table*. London, Michael Joseph.

Liebes, S., Sahtouris, E. and Swimme, B. (1998) *A Walk Through Time: From Stardust to Us*. New York, NY, John Wiley.

Livio, M. (2000) *The Accelerating Universe*. New York, NY, John Wiley and Sons.

Lloyd, G. (1989) The Man of Reason. In *Women, Knowledge and Reality*, A.P. Garry and Marilyn Pearsall (eds). London, Unwin: 111–128.

Lovelock, J. (1991) *Gaia, The Practical Science of Planetary Medicine*. London, Gaia Books.

McDannell, C. and Lang, B. (2001) *Heaven: a History*. New Haven, CT, Yale University Press.

McLeish, K. (1996) *Myth: Myths and Legends of the World Explored*. London, Bloomsbury.

McNeill, J.R. (2000) *Something New Under The Sun: An Environmental History of the Twentieth-Century World*. New York, NY and London, W.W. Norton.

Margulis, L. (1986) *Microcosmos: Four Billion Years of Microbial Evolution*. Berkeley, CA, University of California Press.

Margulis, L. and Sagan, D. (1995) *What is Life?* London, Weidenfeld & Nicholson.

Merchant, C. (1980) *The Death of Nature: Women, Ecology and the Scientific Revolution*. New York, NY, Harper and Row.

Midgley, M. (1989) *Wisdom, Information and Wonder*. London, Routledge.

Midgley, M. (1992) *Science as Salvation: A Modern Myth and Its Meaning*. London and New York, NY, Routledge.

Milton, K. (2002) *Loving Nature: Towards an Ecology of Emotion*. London and New York, NY, Routledge.

Naess, A. (1989) *Ecology, Community and Lifestyle*. Cambridge, Cambridge University Press.

Nelson, S.A. (1998) *God and the Land: The Metaphysics of Farming in Hesiod and Vergil*. Oxford and New York, NY, Oxford University Press.

Nhat Hanh, T. (1988) *The Sun My Heart*. Berkeley, CA, Parallax.

Noble, D.F. (1992) *World Without Women: the Christian Clerical Culture of Western Science*. Oxford and New York, NY, Oxford University Press.

Oberman, H. (1986) *The Dawn of the Reformation: Essays in Late Medieval and Early Reformation Thought*. Edinburgh, T & T Clark.

O'Kelly, M. (1982) *Newgrange, Archaelogy, Art and Legend*. London, Thames and Hudson.

Osserman, R. (1995) *Poetry of the Universe: a Mathematical Exploration of the Cosmos*. New York, NY, Doubleday.

Pagels, E. (1990) *Adam, Eve and the Serpent*. London, Penguin.

Penrose, R. (2002) Interview with Sir Roger Penrose: Part 2. *Mathematics Today*: 13–18.

Perkins, M.A. (1994) *Coleridge's Philosophy: The Logos as Unifying Principle*. Oxford, Clarendon Press.

Peterson, A.L. (2001) *Being Human: Ethics, Environment and Our Place in the World*. Berkeley, CA, University of California Press.

Plumwood, V. (1993) *Feminism and the Mastery of Nature*. London and New York, NY, Routledge.

Polanyi, M. (1958) *Personal Knowledge: Towards a Post-Critical Philosophy*. London, Routledge.

Popkin, R.H. (1977) Spinoza and La Peyrère. *Southwestern Journal of Philosophy* 8: 182–192.

Primavesi, A. (1991) *From Apocalypse to Genesis: Ecology, Feminism and Christianity*. Tunbridge Wells, Burns & Oates.

Primavesi, A. (1998) Gaia Theory and Environmental Policy. In *Spirit of the Environment*, D.E. Cooper and J.A. Palmer (eds). London, Routledge.

Primavesi, A. (2000) *Sacred Gaia*. London and New York, NY, Routledge.

Primavesi, A. (2001a) The Christian Gene. *The Fourth R* 14(3): 3–8.

Primavesi, A. (2001b) Ecology and Christian Hierarchy. In *Women as Sacred Custodians of the Earth?*, Alaine Low and Soraya Tremayne (eds). New York, NY and Oxford, Berghahn Books: 121–140.

Primavesi, A. (2002) The Wisdom of Gaia. *Irish Journal of Feminist Studies* 4: 16–31.

Primavesi, A. and Henderson, J. (1989) *Our God Has No Favourites: A Liberation Theology of the Eucharist*. Tunbridge Wells, Burns & Oates.

Ricoeur, P. (1995) *Figuring the Sacred*. Minneapolis, MN, Fortress.

Rilke, R.M. (1961) *Duino Elegies*. Berkeley and Los Angeles, CA, University of California Press.

Rilke, R.M. (1975) *Poems from the Book of Hours*. New York, NY, New Directions.

Roberts, E. and Amidon, E. (eds) (1991) *Earth Prayers From Around the World*. New York, NY, HarperCollins.

Rose, S. (1998) *Genesis: An Introduction*. Edinburgh, Canongate Books.

Russell, J.B. (1997) *A History of Heaven*. Princeton, NJ, Princeton University Press.

Sagan, C. (1997) *Billions and Billions*. New York, NY, Ballantine.

Scholder, K. (1990) *The Birth of Modern Critical Theology*. London, SCM.

Schroedinger, E. (2000) *What is Life?* Cambridge, Cambridge University Press.

Southgate, C. (2001) Review: Sacred Gaia: Holistic Theology and Earth System Science. *Reviews in Religion and Theology* 8(3): 309–311.

Stevens, W. (2000) *Collected Poems*. New York, NY, Alfred A. Knopf.

Sturgeon, N. (1997) *Ecofeminist Natures: Race, Gender, Feminist Theory and Political Action*. London, Routledge.

Tattersall, I. (1998) *Becoming Human: Evolution and Human Uniqueness*. New York, NY, Harcourt Brace and Company.

Thomas, L. (1975) *The Lives of a Cell: Notes of a Biology Watcher*. New York, NY and London, Bantam Books.

Tolkien, J.R.R. (1968) *The Lord of the Rings*. London, Allen and Unwin.

Volk, T. (2002) *What is Death? A Scientist Looks at the Cycle of Life*. New York, NY, John Wiley and Sons.

von Cues, N. (1957) *Die Kunst der Vermutung*. Bremen, Carl Schuenemann Verlag.

Wackernagel, M. and Rees, W. (1996) *Our Ecological Footprint: Reducing Human Impact on the Earth*. Gabriola Island, BC, New Society Publishers.

Wakeford, T. (2001) *Liaisons of Life*. New York, NY, John Wiley.

Weil, S. (ed.) (1987) *Formative Writings 1929–1941*. London, Routledge.

Westman, R. (ed.) (1975) *The Copernican Achievement*. Berkeley, CA, University of California Press.

Whitman, W. (1926) *Poems*. London, Chatto and Windus.

Yates, F. (1991) *Giordano Bruno and the Hermetic Tradition*. Chicago and London, University of Chicago Press.

Ziman, J. (2000) *Real Science: What It Is, and What It Means*. Cambridge, Cambridge University Press.

Index